Dating Benji

Straight Talk on Improving Your Relationship with Money

By Dasarte Yarnway

Dedication

This book is dedicated to Lonbaye W. Yarnway, Sr. and Moses W. Yarnway, my father and brother. I pray that they rest in peace.

About the Author

Dasarte Yarnway is the cofounder & CEO of Berknell Financial Group. In his role, Dasarte leads the Berknell advisory team and handles investment strategies across client groups. Dasarte has passion for investment management and retirement planning and has spent his career working with clients to design and implement comprehensive planning strategies.

Before the establishment of Berknell Financial Group, Dasarte worked at Fisher Investments and Edward Jones Investments. His most recent stint was as a Vice President, Premier Relationship Advisor, for HSBC Securities, the third largest bank in the world by assets. Through these work experiences, he has concluded that a firm's trusting clients deserve a wealth management process that puts them first.

Dasarte holds the following licenses: Series 7 and Series 66, and he is licensed in multiple states as a life and health insurance producer. Additionally, he is a candidate for the CERTIFIED FINANCIAL PLANNER ™ (CFP) designation.

Dasarte grew up in San Francisco, CA and graduated from the University of California, Berkeley where he lettered on the university's football team. As one of San Francisco's few nationally recognized high school football All-American candidates, he took this opportunity to commit his life and achievements to helping people see the array of possibilities that were available for their lives if they committed to their purpose. Dasarte claims that he is in the 'people business' and on a mission to empower individuals to improve their lives. He insists that financial literacy and planning is just one of the ways to do so. He currently resides in Washington, DC and enjoys fitness, playing golf, and spending time with family.

Acknowledgements

*D*ating Benji started off as an idea—an idea that was stuck in my head for a very long time. I battled with the possibility of writing a book, and I wondered exactly how it would get done and if anyone would read it, but because I know so many people struggle with their relationship with money, it would have hurt me to not put my pen to pad. So I began to write and as the recollections of clients, prospects, friends and family filled my head *Dating Benji* was born.

I would not have been able to finish this book without the help of my mother, Tinniziee and five sisters. They have continually supported me and uplifted me through my most trying times. I would like to thank my business partner and the entire Berknell Financial Group for trusting my leadership and sticking to the challenging duty of truly putting our clients first. Their sweat equity does not go unnoticed. As we persist, Berknell Financial Group will have the opportunity to help millions of people nationwide improve their relationship with money.

Dasarte Yarnway

Special thanks to all of the numerous coaches, friends, neighbors, mentors and communities that have rallied behind me and given me the strength to continue.

Table of Contents

The Love Story

"All is fair in love and war."

Whether we acknowledge it or not, one thing that every human being desires is to be loved. I mean, really. Look around. You probably can't even watch television for 2 hours without an online dating commercial or thinking about your significant other. How about when your text tone lets you know that you received a new text message? You quickly reach for it, only to find out that it's just your co-worker or class-mate asking questions about work or classroom subject matter. Your excitement suddenly fades, doesn't it?

Love. This simple four-letter word comes in a variety of forms, shapes and sizes. Sometimes it makes us shout or jump for joy, and it even forces tears of happiness. In the cold moments of love, we tend to feel weak, vulner-able, depressed or even anxious. Love is a thing that we yearn for passionately, and it controls much of our emo-tions, thoughts, and in some cases, our health and well-ness.

Why does love do this? I'm a finance guy, so I'm not going to try and fool you into thinking that I'm a love ex-pert and that I have all the answers to this game called love. I don't. But, if there is one thing I do know, it is that we all yearn for quality relationships, both intimate and non-intimate. I could lie to you and say that love isn't a big deal and that dating is irrelevant, but even the most pessimistic realists would argue differently. Love is essentially what makes the world go around. Before the physicists come from behind closed doors, let me clarify. Relationships give birth to everything good and bad around us.

Do you remember your first date? You were probably young and eager to make an impression. As your palms sweated, you went back and forth in your head about what the activity would be. Maybe it was dinner and a movie. Maybe you two decided to take a walk in the park. No matter what the outing was, you tried to showcase your best self. You wanted to make sure that none of your flaws were on display and that you presented yourself as a viable candidate for a relationship—a good catch.

Now, do you remember your first relationship? Not second, third, or for some, your marriage. I'm talking about your first intimate relationship. Think about it. For most of us, it was here that we developed our own understanding of the symbiotic nature of relationships. At this time, you began to formulate your understanding of what a relationship was and your standard for a romantic partner. You probably could have described yourself as full of potential. You were likely young, dumb, and ripe for a plethora of mistakes. This relationship taught you about yourself. It brought out your strengths and weaknesses and it encouraged you to truly develop into the best you that you could be.

This relationship taught you how to care deeply for another person, to accept their inequities and to try to love unconditionally. It also taught you that you are not perfect. It taught you that there were things about you that you could work on and that you have to love yourself first before you could unselfishly love anyone else.

In reflecting on this relationship, it's fair to say that you made a lot of mistakes. Some might describe their behavior in that relationship as selfish. Others might think that they were immature, or even go as far as saying that they simply weren't ready. Oftentimes, we take those experiences and we learn from them, resulting in a change of behavior in relationships that follow. In the proceeding relationships, you can now feel when the baggage claim begins to revolve and release the old behavior and emotions that you have worked so hard to grow away from. That realization alone is a sign of growth because now you consciously choose your behavior and are able to decipher between what is right and what is wrong. You've gained the power of free will!

This relationship is much like the relationship that you have with your personal finances. You are reading this book because you want to take everything that you learned in the past about yourself and enter into a new relationship with your money matters. We could begin to reflect on our former relationship with money in our childhood where we were given an allowance and quickly realized that money provided us with options for food and candy. Perhaps we could start during our teenage years when we might have begun to understand the money matters of our parents. Bills had to be paid, and some of us watched things fail to be paid. For some of us, our parents began to harp on the importance of saving and being responsible with money in our early adolescent years.

I prefer to start at the point of acknowledgement. This happens at different times for different people. For some, acknowledgement might have occurred at your first job when you were asked by the human resources department how much you wanted to contribute to your 401(k) and you didn't know what to do. Maybe it was when you turned 35 with an extremely successful career, but didn't have much aside from "things" to show for it. Acknowledgement could occur on your 50th birthday when you might reflect on your life and retirement plan, and you notice that your individual retirement accounts (IRAs) do not match the dream that you envisioned. No matter when your point of acknowledgement was, this book aims to help you identify your downfalls, but more importantly, position you for future success with your relationship with money.

Meet Benjamin. The truth is you have had a changing relationship with Benjamin, or Benji. You've observed elders using Benji to buy groceries, toys, give you allowances, and even as a means for punishment. You've been excited over finding a few dollars under your pillow when you lost a tooth, and even tried to save them in a piggy bank once upon a time. Benji has paid for your tuition, even if you had to earn him yourself, and has allowed you to take trips overseas. He might have even helped you earn a spot as the life of the party when you and your friends have hit the town. As you can see, Benjamin's influence is all around us and has been for quite some time.

Your image of Benjamin has walked alongside you and has changed over the years just as you have. As you reach new milestones in life, your depiction of money and its use will inevitably change again.

The issue that most of us have when it comes to our relationship with Benjamin is that we let him control us. We owe a large amount of Benjamins after graduating from college. We stress over how to make more Benjis once we've cleared our debt. We even do things that we hate just because it may offer a few more coins than something that we absolutely love. As we edge closer towards retirement, we begin to dread the process of planning on how to properly save our money, and most times, we don't have a clear strategy for Benjamin in retirement. And let's not even get on the subject of "feeling broke." In these cases, we may even wage war with our own loved ones because Benjamin has topped the list on our hierarchy of values, causing us to lose sight of the people and things that are priceless.

Our relationship with money can be a double-edged sword, but only if we make it that way. Instead of letting money divide our families, cause stress, and blur our vision, it can be used as something that offers us experiences, makes our goals realities, and fast tracks our children to a life that we may have never had. *In reality, there is only one truth in our relationship with Benjamin: he never changes, only the way that we use him does.* If you are able to truly understand this fact, you are halfway to improving your relationship with money.

You are about to read a book that is going to change the way that you think about money. And no, I am not speaking of the redundant clamor of stocks, bonds, and annualized return. I am speaking of tapping into your relationship with the greenbacks that we toil for day in and day out.

I'm a strong believer that we are not fully responsible for our views and relationships with money. It's not your fault. The good news is that changing your partnership with money is not rocket science, but that does not mean that it is easy. If it were, we would all be committed to our financial plans, have enough money for retirement, and enjoy the fruits of our discipline all because we made one choice: the choice inside of our heads to improve our relationship with Benjamin.

This book is your counsel to tap into improving your current financial situation—no matter where you are in life, career, or circumstance:

- This book will help you identify your dating down-falls.
- This book will help you identify your money personality.
- This book will help you reflect on your values with your relationship with money.
- This book with give you guidelines on how to approach financial planning.
- This book will help you be more goal-oriented in your desires versus dollar-oriented. It's different from your average finance book because the foundation starts with your relationship with money and not with money itself.
- This book will give you guidelines for finding relationship coaches.
- This book is for you. Not everyone majors in finance, works in the financial services industry, or has an interest in understanding the inner workings of capital markets. This book is for the person who simply wants to put one foot in front of the other toward financial security.

Like in your intimate relationships, without proper guidance and exposure to healthy relationships, it was inevitable that you would make a few mistakes. *Dating Benji* seeks to heal those wounds and correct your mistakes through acknowledgement, education and proper planning infrastructure.

With this, let us begin our journey. May your new relationship be much better than your last.

Part 1: The Dating Downfalls

"Honesty is the best policy when there's money in it."

L et's go back to the first relationship of yours. Scratch that. I'll use myself as the example here. I remember being a young man and so in love. Oh yeah. If you asked me if I was marrying this woman, undoubtedly, my answer would have been a resounding yes. It was too good to be true at times. In my mind, with that type of intense desire, the stars would align and the universe would conspire to grant us everything that we wished for.

Well, I was wrong. Although in a relationship where we thought we heard weddings bells, the stars aligned pushing us in a direction that didn't result in marriage. It resulted in self-improvement. There were many things that we needed to improve upon both individually and collectively if we ever wanted the relationship to become a holy union. Now, I'm fine with that.

The divorce rate in the United States of America is a staggering 50 percent. That means that there is a one out of two chance that after saying "I do," you and your partner may not end as planned. That's a scary statistic. Can you guess what the number one reason for divorce is in our country? Maybe I've made it a little too easy for you. You guessed it. The number one reason for divorce in the U.S. is the lack of communication. In a close second comes the lack of transparency about personal finances. Like the lack of communication, your personal financial matters have "dating downfalls" that can obstruct your growth. Let's outline the three dating downfalls that most people face with their personal financial planning.

Dating Downfall #1:
The Abuse of Consumer Credit

Credit may very well be the root of all evil. In all seriousness, when it comes to financial responsibility, the abuse of credit is the Achilles' heel of many men. We've all heard of or used credit before. The credit card dates its origins back to the 1800s. It was used as a medium for consumers and merchants to exchange goods. Only about one hundred years ago was the credit card introduced in the plastic form that we are used to today.

I like to think of the credit card as a double-edge sword, which makes its use pivotal to its holder. On one end, you can use credit to build a great reputation with merchants and large institutions for timely payments of the balance of the credit they extend to you to purchase goods and services. Thus, they provide you with more options and a larger spending limit. On the other end of the spectrum, with the abuse of consumer credit, you consequently build a bad reputation with merchants and lending institutions and are considered untrustworthy.

This in turn limits your options for purchases such as a home and car. The largest pain of this behavior is the immense pressure of collection agencies that may be hired on behalf of the merchants and institutions to recover the money that was extended by them. If the collection agencies are not calling you, a benign stressor may be the fact that you will now be paying minimum payments for a very, very long time.

Let's analyze. You walked into Best Buy to purchase a 60-inch flat screen television. You begin to pace up and down the aisles in the television section looking for the perfect wall unit for your living room. After speaking with the sales representative, you find that the price of a flat screen smart television meeting your specific criteria will range anywhere from $1,600 to $2,400.

You continue to nag the sales associates. Besides, you have to make sure that Monday night football is viewed in high definition clarity and that your wife won't have a problem recording her favorite reality TV show when she's not home. After hearing the associate's final pitch, you come to the conclusion that the picture quality, sounds, app capabilities and resolutions of two models all meet your standards. Check.

Will it be the Vizio or the Toshiba? Decisions, decisions. The Vizio brand will cost you $2,400 and is at the top of your budget, while the Toshiba will cost you $2,000. After the long wallet waltz, you've made your decision, and the Vizio television is coming back home with you for $2,400.

Here's the part where credit gets involved. There are now three ways for you to purchase this item: cash, or debit or credit. Hypothetically, you could initiate a cash purchase by shelling out 24 single hundred dollar bills from your wallet, one-by-one, until you've reached the grand total. The thing about this option that most people hate is that midway through the exchange of cash, they're reminded of the price of their purchase. Emotionally, watching any amount, especially a large amount, of your hard-earned money leave your hands and fall into another person's is just too painful. $2,400? Ouch.

If that doesn't fit your payment taste, you could choose the option to pay in the form of debit. Debit is a cash transaction, but it won't hurt as much as handing over twenty-four paperbacks. You see, when we use our debit cards for purchases, we have the convenience of swiping our cards quickly, saving us from the emotional distress of seeing the money go, but we now have the task of checking for damage control at a later date. The good part about it is you will not harm your credit score in the process. The bad part is you could find yourself stretched for cash without a budget.

Your last option and most common is the credit payment. Let me note that most people have healthy intentions when they initiate a payment using their credit cards. They say to themselves, "I'm going to use it this one time, and I'm going to pay off the entire balance at the end of the month," but the allure of minimum payments often prevails in the event of a cash flow crunch. Now, back to the purchase. Instead of handing over the cold hard cash or using the debit card, you pull out your credit card and hand it over to the associate at the register. Beep! You swipe it, get the approval and within minutes, you are out the door and on your way home with a brand new 60-inch Vizio television, cash still in your checking account, and an obligation to pay only a portion of the cost per month.

Like the lack of communication in our romantic relationships, oftentimes, relying on credit cards without aggressively paying down the balance leads us down a path of disconnect with our financial situations. It's very convenient to not communicate the things that may hurt us most with our romantic relationships. The same emotional compromise happens when we swipe our plastic payment mechanisms without the funds to aggressively pay off the balances towards the end of the month. Emotionally, it's just easier, and Benji doesn't appreciate shortcuts.

Dating Downfall #2: Failing to Pay Yourself First

One of my favorite saving quotes to date is by Warren Buffett. In an interview, the investment guru is asked a multitude of questions about personal finance, investing, his company Berkshire Hathaway and keys to managing one's assets. On the subject of saving, Buffett states, "Do not save what is left after spending, but spend what it left after saving."

Stop. Think. How much better would our financial lives be if we followed this guideline more times than not? If you have this mentality already, then I applaud you. If not, then your savings account and balances may reflect your disobedience to Buffett's rule.

It is estimated that the average American will need 60 to 80 percent of their annual salary yearly to live a comfortable retirement. Let's use Joe as an example. Joe makes $100,000 per year and is employed as a software engineer for a reputable tech company headquartered in the San Francisco Bay Area. By the standards of most, Joe lives a good life, and by good life, I mean that he has a lot of nice things: a loft in downtown San Jose, a new BMW, designer clothes and is not short of frequent flyer miles. From his salary, Joe's 401(k) contribution is three percent with an employer match of three percent of his salary.

Okay, are you lost yet? No? Good. At Joe's contribution rate, he is putting away $3,000 per year. If you include his employer's contribution, at this rate, his annual grand total is $6,000 in contribution, not including any return on investment. Assuming a modest rate of return of five percent in this first year of his contribution, he'll make a modest 300 bucks on his initial investment of $6,000.

If we take our general expectation into consideration, Joe will need at least $60,000 per year to live comfortably in retirement.

With his reoccurring expenses and a non-existing emergency fund, Joe has fallen victim to the net income trap, otherwise known as the failure to pay yourself first. Nowadays, most people do not receive paper paycheck stubs. In the direct deposit age, it is more difficult to pinpoint and evaluate the deductions and contributions that come out of your paycheck.

Let's assess. On what used to be your paycheck stub, there are a series of deductions, taxations and contributions that are outlined. These are your 401(k) contributions, federal and state taxes, social security (FICA) taxes, disability insurance and health and dental deductions. Whew! In regards to paying yourself, your 401(k) deduction is a starting point for treating Benji the way he deserves to be treated. The issue is we tend to fall in love with the net number, and not the number we pay ourselves. Because of this, we choose to contribute less, spend more on the things that we presently want, and eventually come around to saving. This is a major dating downfall.

Like in any relationship, the connection, whether good or bad, will only develop with time. Retirement saving relies heavily on a concept in finance known as the time value of money. Time value of money suggests that the present money available is worth more in the future than its current amount due to compound interest. This principle proves that any amount of money is worth more the sooner that it is invested. In essence, time is on your side. In your 401(k), your assets will grow over time. With systematic contributions, you will only inch closer and possibly exceed the general requirement of 60 to 80 percent of your annual salary, helping you live a long, enjoyable retirement.

As for your net amount, a portion of that should go towards your emergency fund, which we will touch on in detail later in our straight talk. If you remember anything from dating downfall number two, remember this: Paying yourself first should be seen as a necessity along the lines of breathing or drinking water. After, and only after, paying yourself first should you spend money on the other necessities of life.

Dating Downfall #3:
Living Above Your Means

As the saying goes, first impressions are lasting impressions. The cool part about dating Benji is that even if your first impression is horrible, he gives you the time and the room to make improvements. What a sweetheart!

Everyone has been on this type of date: the impression date. What's the impression date, you ask? The impression date has all of the bells and whistles such as an expensive dinner or activity, and it takes away from the substance and synergy that the two individuals are trying to explore. While nice, the finer things may almost be a distraction from what you are looking for. Regardless of what the impression tool was, oftentimes, the lavish nature of the gesture is not a necessity for building a relationship. If you like her in a classy restaurant, you would probably like her on a walk through the park. If you like enjoying a couples' massage with him, you would likely enjoy a cup of coffee with him too.

A *Dating Benji* downfall is when we decide, whether consciously or unconsciously, to live above our means.

Today, we minimize the phenomenon to a phrase, "living paycheck to paycheck." Remember our friend Joe? Well, as illustrated in dating downfall number two, he sacrifices paying himself first to pay for other things, which buys him a membership in the paycheck-to-paycheck club.

The relationship between paying ourselves first and living above or within our means is much like the correlation of certain downfalls in our intimate relationships. Let's use dishonesty as an example. Have you ever caught your significant other being dishonest about something? At the time, you probably had a gut feeling that something just wasn't right. You didn't want to look like the crazy, untrusting partner either, so you battled on whether to express your feelings or to wait until the signs were clear or not. When you received the empirical data necessary to address the situation, you did. Maybe you forgave your partner, maybe you didn't. Nonetheless, your heart was broken and you acquired a lack of trust toward the individual and, potentially, towards a new love that had nothing to do with the incident. Typically, these two *Dating Benji* downfalls come in a package.

Back to Joe. We know that Joe is the victim of the net-income trap. Remember all of the cool things that Joe had: the beamer, the downtown rented loft and designer clothing? Well, it ain't cheap. Rent at the downtown location costs $1,950 per month. His car note on his luxury vehicle costs $350 per month, not to mention his discretionary spending budget of $250. His designer shopping budget is $500 per month with a utility bill of $125. Wait, there's more. Joe's cable bill tops off at $100 per month with a food and gas bill of about $400 per month. After all of that, he owes Sallie Mae $300 per month, pays a life insurance premium of $200 and his credit card balance of $250. Whew! Deep breaths. Now, say it with me, "I am bigger than my expenses." Good.

Here's Joe's expense breakdown:

Rent: $1,950

Car Note: $350

Shopping: $500

Discretionary Budget: $250

Utilities: $125

Cable: $100

Food & Gas: $400

Life Insurance: $200

Credit Card: $250

Student Loans: $300

Total Monthly Expenses: $4,425

It wouldn't be fair of me to just show you Joe's personal expenses without showing you his income breakdown. Below is Joe's bi-weekly income statement. It takes into consideration federal and state income taxes, social security tax, Medicare, his 401(k) contribution and state disability insurance.

Bi-Weekly Gross Pay: $3,846.15

Federal Tax Withholding: $752.57

Social Security Tax: $231.31

Medicare: $54.10

State (CA) Tax: $258.98

SDI: $34.62

401(k): $115.38

Bi-Weekly Net: $2,399.19

Monthly Net Pay: 4,798.38

After all of his expenses, Joe is left with $373.38. In the best case scenario, he'll save all of the cash left over, and he'll have a total annual savings of a little north of $4,000 per year. Best. Case. Scenario. In a world of rainy days, gift purchases and spur-of-the-moment decisions, it's safe to say that keeping that kind of discipline would be hard for many of us. We're only human; we are bound to make mistakes.

The concerning aspect of Joe's situation is that at 40 years of age, even if he saved $4,000 per year from now until his full retirement age of 65, he would only have $100,000 in savings. With the addition of his $6,000 per year 401(k) contribution and its growth, we can conservatively tack on an additional $150,000, give or take, with the fluctuations in his returns. Still, it would be impossible for Joe to distribute $60,000 per year to live on in retirement without running out of money. Benji says 'save me now and I'll save you later.' This brief summary alone shows that not paying himself first and living above his means will make life extremely hard down the line.

Lifestyle inflation is something that over 60 percent of Americans fall victim to. It is a binding habit that is debilitating to your future financial wellness. By definition, lifestyle inflation is simply the increase of spending as your income increases. Every time a person gets a raise and boosts their spending, they make it difficult to pay off debt, pay themselves first, and plan for other long-term financial goals. We all know the Joneses. Trying to keep up with them encourages lifestyle inflation.

The better approach would be to assess our lifestyle needs both currently and in the future using three categories: needs, wants and wishes. By doing this, we align our goals and budgets with our pocketbooks saving us from the dating downfall that is living above our means. This practice of prioritizing is by no means an easy task. Utilizing a budget can help monitor income, expenses and spending patterns. A budget can be prepared from using the amount of your income and expenditures in the recent past and should be updated and reviewed periodically. It should consider your goals, immediate needs and future needs.

The two most important pieces that your budget will disclose to you are your discretionary and nondiscretionary income. Your nondiscretionary income is a recurring or nonrecurring expense that a person has to maintain their lifestyle. Right now for Joe, three examples of non-discretionary expenses would be his monthly rent payment, car note and utilities. Discretionary income is a recurring or nonrecurring expense for a good or service that isn't essential to uphold a person's lifestyle. Examples of these expenses for Joe would be his $500 monthly shopping expense and his "bar budget" of $250. These things are not necessities and can be put to better use for Joe.

The discipline required to consistently use credit appropriately, pay yourself first and budget is extremely challenging. In fact, I would compare it to the training that athletes have to endure to reach their goals on the playing field. Muhammad Ali was once quoted saying, "I hated every minute of training, but I said, 'Don't quit. Suffer now and live the rest of your life as a champion.'" Unlike Ali, if you think of saving for your own benefit as suffering, it'll be much more difficult to achieve the task. Don't suffer, prioritize. Living within your means isn't the glamorous thing to do, especially when most of America is doing the exact opposite. Doing so could ensure that you have the resources available to live in the way that you always dreamt at one of the most crucial times in your life. You'll thank yourself later.

In our relationships, sometimes knowing what the downfalls are beforehand steers us away from hurting ourselves and hurting others. If we still participate in the dating downfalls after learning of them, it now becomes a conscious choice, and that is no one's fault but your own. It's up to you to make the right choice.

Questions That Need Answers

1. Which of the dating downfalls have you fallen victim to? Why?

_____

_____

_____

_____

_____

2. What steps have you taken to correct your downfall?

_____

_____

_____

_____

_____

3. Are you utilizing your employer-sponsored retirement accounts? If so, do you think you are paying yourself enough?

_____

_____

_____

_____

_____

4. Does your use of credit work for you or against you?

_____

_____

_____

_____

_____

Part 2: Getting Your Groove Back

"Someone is sitting under a tree that someone else planted many years ago."

S adness. For most people, sadness is one of the first emotions felt when two people decide to go their separate ways. Sharing a significant amount of time with a person translates into a rolodex of memories—both good and bad. Coming to the realization that memories with this person are no longer strikes a chord with our emotions and requires time for us to heal, or as some would say, time to "get over it." Whether it takes 3 months or 3 years, it takes time to understand your role in contributing to the breakup and to answer any lingering questions. Think about it. You get upset when you lose $20, so losing a person, better yet, a friend, hurts 10 times worse. This experience is known as the reflection period.

The dating downfalls discussed in Part 1 and the questions that needed answers serve as a period to reflect on some of the strengths and weaknesses that you may have had in your former relationship with money. The key to the transition point after the period of reflection lies with the answer to one question: Will you choose to carry the mental baggage from your old relationship with Benji into your new one?

We see this all the time in our own romantic relationships or, perhaps, the relationships of friends or family members. How many times do we learn lessons from our relationships, and instead of using those lessons to be a better version of ourselves for a deserving person, and more importantly ourselves, we take our baggage into our new relationship?

Was it the girl that said she would not marry you after years of sharing your life with her? Could it have been the guy that that couldn't fully commit to you? Perhaps it was the person that just did not want something serious. Whatever it was, this situation causes us to close our minds and our hearts to the possibilities of love and intimacy. If you are going to carry the mental pain from your previous dating downfalls into your new relationship with Benji, I encourage you to stop reading now. Yup. That's right. You can close the book right now and continue on the path that you may have been on before. That may sound harsh, but let me explain.

Sometimes in our relationships, we find ourselves wasting the time of the people that we are attracted to. Often, individuals rush the reflection process when they are just not ready. They are still attached to the pain that they felt from losing a partner, loved one, or a friend.

They're hurt. In our relationships, we can massage our pain with someone else's emotions, but the inevitable result is a waste of time and a broken heart in the process. The same rule applies for the pursuit of a relationship with Benji. Too often after ended relationships, we want the perks of love without the discipline and vulnerability that is required. You can't expect a healthy relationship with Benji with unhealthy relationship habits. It does not work like that in love and it certainly does not work like that if you plan on improving your relationship with Benji. After this period of reflection, it's time to get your groove back.

Know Thyself

When improving your relationship with Benji, it starts with knowing yourself. You've reflected, identified your strengths and weaknesses and committed to leaving the past in the past. From all of your analysis, you've now developed a money personality. This serves as your general identification for your actions and behaviors.

The Myers-Briggs personality indicator is widely recognized as one of the leading personality tests in many countries. Based on Carl Jung's groundbreaking research, Isabel Briggs Myers and her mother Katharine Cook Briggs developed the Myers-Briggs Type Indicator, a reflective, self-assessment designed to pinpoint psychological attributes of how people view the world and make decisions. Carl Jung's typographical theory speculates that humans experience the universe in four key ways. These ways are intuition, logic or thinking, sensation and feeling. The Myers-Briggs Type Indicator takes Jung's theory and suggests that we all have specific characteristics in the way that we construct and construe our values, and our particular approach reflects our values, interests and needs.

The Myers-Briggs Type Indicator offers 16 distinct personality types that resonate with millions of people worldwide. When it comes to money matters, there are five different personality types that can summarize the behaviors of individuals within their relationship with Benji. Which one are you?

The Five Money Personalities

The Big Saver

Big Savers are typically people who search through what most would view as junk mail for attractive deals.

They cut out coupons for weekly savings and make sure that the front and refrigerator doors are not left ajar in order to conserve energy. They save everything! These money conscious individuals typically only carry necessary debt such as home and student loans. Many people mistake them as "cheap." Unbothered by the latest fads, they are more aroused by monitoring the upward movement of their credit scores and seeing a tiny bit of interest accumulate on their bank statements. In the minds of the Big Saver, it's about not being careless and not losing money.

People also tend to mistake the Big Saver as conservative, but in reality, they are just risk adverse. Their motto is: "Why spend it or risk it when you can just save it?" The security in knowing that their money is safe and abundant is far more important than growth, experiences and compound interest.

The Big Spender

The Big Spender has been commercialized in our society since what seems like the beginning of time. In movies, the Big Spender is typically the guy that sits at the roulette table, bets big and captivates the crowd's attention. He could also be the romantic that takes you on a lavish first date or purchases a gaudy ring. The Big Spender can be the woman who only wears expensive designer clothes and shops at the priciest of grocery stores. No matter what they're spending it on, this money personality has no problem reaching into their wallet.

With their "you only live once" attitudes, it is almost a guarantee that when the Big Spender is around, they are the life of the party. They not only spend, but encourage others to understand that they can't take their cash with them when they are gone. For the Big Spender, life is far too short to penny pinch. They see the spending of their money as their way of enjoying life, showing affection, and as a reward for all of the hard work that they have put in over the years, weeks, months or hours. In their eyes, the opportunity cost of missing out on an experience is way more than the price of the experience itself. This belief is the reason why the Big Spender is not out looking for a bargain. This money personality is more identifiable to the naked eye than any other personality.

Big Spenders love nice things because these render new experiences. Everything that they do is big! This personality likes brand name clothing, the newest technology and fine automobiles. There's no need to keep up with the Joneses because Big Spenders are the Joneses and take pride in the things that make them so. They are not afraid of debt and have a higher risk tolerance towards markets and investing. Deep down, they know that they should be doing something better with their money, but they would hate to relinquish the lifestyle that they and, often, their families have gotten used to, because you only live once, right?

The Free Spirit

The Free Spirit is the most interesting personality of all. If I could put my finger on this personality, it reminds me of the friend or lover who is always up for a new adventure. Today, they want to spontaneously book a one-way trip to Europe. In a couple of weeks, another career change is on the horizon, and last month, they picked up their third new hobby of the year—and it was only March.

Generally, they are not as connected to their money as the Big Saver, but are not as loose as the Big Spender. The Free Spirit is an individual who simply isn't giving much thought to how they spend their money and their relationship with Benji. Their decisions are based heavily on feeling and intuition. Because money matters are not a top priority, the Free Spirit is usually unaware and unprepared when planning for their financial future.

In most cases, this money personality spends more money than they earn and carries above average debt due to their lack of accounting. Free Spirits rarely think about investing and view money as just a means to do the things that they'd like to do at any given moment in time. This personality is intriguing because of their skewed nature towards either the Big Saver or Spender and greatly benefit from having a budget and sound financial plan.

The Conservative

The Conservative is often mistaken for the Big Saver, and for good reason, as the two personalities often demonstrate similar characteristics. These money personalities are very tactical with their purchases and debts. They do a great job of outlining their needs, wants and wishes, and doing so in a way that is rational and cost-effective. Conservatives, in a money sense, are defined as individuals who want to participate in the growth, experiences and compound interest with limited risk, while the Big Saver is completely allergic to risk.

Because of this, Conservatives find themselves comfortable having loads of money in their low-rate "high-yield" savings accounts at banks because of the FDIC's insurability on the money and the risk. The problem is that they often find themselves in a position demanding them to take more risks later in life to make up for returns that they missed out on while their money was liquid.

For this reason, the Conservative benefits from a transparent, thorough explanation of the risk reward on investments and why assuming some risk may be necessary for them to reach their financial goals. They benefit greater from a financial advisor who can keep them on track when they experience fluctuations in their investment portfolios.

The Investor

The Investors are the poster children of all the money personalities. This money personality does one thing very well: They see the big picture. They understand that while we all have immediate needs, without planning, appropriate risk and patience, they will never be able to reach their big picture goals. The Investor knows that Benji reciprocates the love that we show to him. To stick to our financial plans and invest the money we make is to love Benji unconditionally. If you do this, Benji will love you back in a way that you've never imagined. The Investors are masters of paying themselves first and building systematic investments, such as monthly or yearly IRA contributions into their budgets. They understand that without risk, there is no reward, and they know their tolerance for risk. Investing isn't a chore for them, but more of a way of life. They seek to diversify their income in the most efficient ways possible, because sometimes, working a job isn't enough. They are forward thinkers.

Perhaps the best quality of the Investors is that they understand the power of time. The Investor knows that time value of money is what will help him or her build, sustain and harvest wealth. They know that eventually, this is the same mechanism that will help them gift assets to their families after they have lived a long, successful life.

The downfall of Investors can be their overconfidence in their craft. They've studied the "how-tos" of investing, so they think that they are experts or can just do it themselves. Because of this, the Investors are prone to taking unnecessary risks and paying with the investment choices and allocations in their portfolio. As the old proverb goes, "A wise man knows that he does not know all things." The Investor has the best of intentions in regards to his personal finances, but needs the guidance to make the right decisions at the right times. Sometimes this money personality needs to be saved from themselves.

In reflecting on your past relationship with money, you should be able to see where your old characteristics align with one of these five relationship types. In being honest with yourself, you'll be able to take the steps necessary to set up your goals which will help you prioritize your needs, wants and wishes.

How to Date Benjamin

It's finally time to start your new relationship with Benjamin. In our romantic relationships, a step that many people forget to address is expectation setting. Setting expectations of each other can help the two parties avoid many of the romantic dating downfalls before it's too late. For example, the free spirit simply may not want a serious relationship. If that's communicated before the courting stage, no feelings get hurt and the counterpart gets to make a decision on whether or not this type of relationship fits what they're looking for. Because Benjamin cannot set expectations for us, we typically do not recognize our failure to set proper expectations of our relationship with money until it is too late. What does too late look like in a relationship with Benji, you ask? Too late is the point at which you have limited the availability of options for your money goals. For example, you began to pay yourself seriously in your company's 401(k) at the age of 50. Your early retirement goals may be too far out of reach for you to save enough money to live through 25 years in retirement without working. Yet, if we set our boundaries and expectations at the onset of our rebirthed relationship with Benji, we can look for appropriate solutions.

Everyone that dates has a motive. Unfortunately, while dating, some people have pure intentions, and others, not so much. The point is no matter the intentions, there is something that both parties want out of the situation. You have goals and everything has a price. Benjamin wants to be used to help you reach your goals, but it's up to you to let him. Whether you have troubles after payday, or have troubles with day-to-day spending, there will be expectations that you will have to hold yourself accountable to, for the truth again is money never changes, only our use of it does. Here are four key points that you will have to analyze to make sure that you are setting proper expectations:

Understand your values. Too often, we spend money on things that we do not value. This leaves us with less and a feeling of emptiness. Seriously dating Benji means that we offer our time and conscious efforts to reach our defined goals. Maybe you value family and making sure that they are protected. Perhaps you value education and would like to help partially pay for your children's tuition. Defining your values is pivotal in planning for their fruition.

Understand yourself. A wise man once said, "Honesty is the best policy when there's money in it." We've acknowledged our dating downfalls, reflected and have identified our money personalities. Benjamin knows that you are coming to him with distinct personality traits that aren't necessarily all positive. This go around, you'll have to accept your strengths and development opportunities that you are bringing to the relationship. Face them head on and watch your goals become more realistic.

Understand your goals. What are your goals for

finding a partner? Do you want to be with someone who wants to work towards marriage? If you are already married, what goals do you and your husband or wife want to share with one another? Maybe you'd like to travel to every continent in retirement or buy a retirement home in Florida. Our use of Benjamin is the variable, and it is imperative that we tie goals to our money matters so that we can blueprint and create solutions to get there.

When planning for goals, people usually start with the number of dollars that they feel is enough to help them reach their goal. This is called a dollar-oriented goal. Saying that you need to retire with one million dollars, but with no specified goal or logic is almost as bad as one of the three dating downfalls because you'll do anything to achieve that number, including all of the wrong things. If you start the planning process with your goals, a clear-cut path of action can be more easily defined and will help you fulfill your money goals.

Be impeccable with your actions. Relationships are the ultimate action sports. With money, you can have the perfect budget, financial plan and investment strategy, but all of that means nothing without action. Your action is the single thing that ties the relationship together. Without an impeccable, actionable plan, you'll never reach your goals and the double-edged sword will continue to pierce you.

Starting Point: Personal Net Worth

Imagine this. You and your significant other have a near perfect relationship. You guys understand each other's personality, and have even talked about each other's past. You've set the expectations and the boundaries for this stage of the relationship and have accepted one another's falls and all. Tonight is date night. The two of you will be dining at your favorite sports bar and watching an NBA game together (talk about being cost-effective). You two pleasantly enjoy the game and the food.

Despite the perfect relationship, a local photographer who has been taking pictures of the event caught you and your significant other in a not so intimate moment. She walks over to show you the picture and it shows both you and your partner paying each other no mind, fiddling with your cell phones. In that still shot, one would not be able to tell that you two were madly in love.

I'm sure that you've heard the term *net worth* bounced around. Nowadays, it comes up in media when sources try to estimate a person's wealth and assets. The net worth concept is a simple measure to assess how much a person or business is worth. To calculate a person's net worth, you simply take all of their assets and subtract their liabilities, which brings you to their net worth. To be even simpler, your net worth is everything that you own minus everything that you've been loaned. Like the picture taken at the sports bar, your net worth can be a viewed as a snapshot of your financial health at any given moment in time. It can help you to pinpoint specific debts and assets that could appreciate over time. Below is a sample personal net worth work sheet:

Personal Net Worth Statement

Assets

Checking Accounts $ _____

Savings Accounts $ _____

Retirement Funds $ _____

Investment Accounts $ _____

Real Estate Holdings $ _____

Other Personal Property $ _____

Other Assets $ _____

Total Assets $ _____

Liabilities

Credit Card Balance $ _____

Auto and Other Loans $ _____

Installment Accounts $ _____

Mortgage Balances $ _____

Loans against Life Insurance $ _____

Other Liabilities $ _____

Total Liabilities $ _____

Net Worth

Total Assets $ _____

Less Total Liabilities $ _____

Net Worth $ _____

If your assets exceed your liabilities, congratulations! You have a positive net worth. Contrarily, if your liabilities exceed your assets, you have a negative net worth. This snapshot will be helpful in pinpointing the start point in your relationship with Benji. It will remind you of dating downfalls if your liabilities are increasing, and it will encourage you when your net worth shifts or increases in positivity. The numbers don't lie, and your net worth statement is the first step before the planning takes place.

Questions That Need Answers

1. What money personality do you identify with most?

   _____

   _____

   _____

   _____

   _____

2. What are your money goals for the future? Are you
   taking the right steps today to achieve those goals?

   _____

   _____

   _____

   _____

   _____

3. Are you impeccable with your actions? Why or why not?

_____

_____

_____

_____

_____

4. Complete the personal net worth work sheet. Do you have a positive or negative personal net worth at this time?

_____

_____

_____

_____

_____

Part 3: The RIITE Planning Process

"Failure to plan is the failure to succeed."

The Smart Phone Map

Finding love is sometimes unpredictable. You never know whom you will meet or what it will take to fall in love. Unfortunately, it usually does not happen as perfectly as it does in the movies. There are many different ways to meet people, ways to build relationships, and some would even say that true love can be found upon first sight.

You likely have a smart phone, and if I had to guess, when you need directions to reach a destination, one of the first things that you do is put the start point and destination into the phone. After this, your smart phone will likely populate a few different options: the fastest route, the scenic route and the route with the least traffic. You may not have familiarity with the road of choice, but getting to the destination is of the highest importance. You pick the one that seems the best for you with hopes of getting to the destination in a safe and timely manner.

In the financial services industry, I have seen many financial institutions and firms make complicated plans and forgettable acronyms without creating a process for their clients to understand the route of choice for their goals. How can you ever improve your relationship with

Benjamin without a plan that you understand?

Because of this void in the industry, I've created an acronym that helps all money personalities clearly view and plan for a better, more fruitful relationship with Benji. The acronym is RIITE, and the process that we use is called the RIITE Planning Process. As stated previously, there are many ways to reach a goal, whether in your romantic relationships or with your money. In using this process, you can now take all of the things that you've learned from this book about yourself and apply goals and numbers to specific planning criteria.

The RIITE Planning Process covers the areas of retirement, insurance, investments, taxes, estate and emergency funds planning—all necessary for financial security and successful financial planning. I'll touch on each aspect of the process to give you tips on how to plan and best practices.

Retirement

Retirement is expensive. A long time ago, retirement assets were seen as a three-legged stool. The three legs were your assets from your company's pension, your individual savings and social security benefits. With pensions becoming more and more of an endangered species, many people are left only with their self-funded company retirement plans, social security benefits, and potentially, an inheritance.

The Department of Labor estimates that less than half of Americans have calculated what they need to save for retirement. Based on their research in 2014, 30 percent of workers who were eligible to participate in an employer-sponsored plan did not participate. As the average American spends near 20 years in retirement, not saving enough could very realistically mean not retiring at all.

Retirement planning can be viewed as cardio exercise. Most of us don't want to do it, but it is very good for our heart health. The benefits of this type of exercise are numerous: increased metabolism, improved hormonal profile and weight management, amongst others. Yet, because the task is so rigorous, we may opt not to do it. We forego the rewards for the convenience of right now. I'll be the first person to tell you that convenience is not worth working five, ten, or even twenty extra years.

So how do you get started exactly? First, learn about your company's retirement plan. How much do they match? How long will you have to stay with the company before you can roll over the entire balance that you've saved? Finding out the specifics could help you plan both for your personal retirement and professionally. Then, contribute! There are many benefits to contributing to your company sponsored retirement plan. The obvious reason is that you are saving and growing assets that would otherwise be spent on things that you won't need 20 years from now. Other perks such as lower taxable income, automatic deductions from your paychecks and employee matches all apply.

If you aren't contributing to your employer sponsored plan, such as a 401(k), you have to start. If you are contributing a small amount, you should consider contributing as much as you can within your means. A rule of thumb is to save 10 to 15 percent of your gross income, which includes any matches from your employer. If you do this early and often, your retirement goals are very much within reach. The time value of money concept proves that the compound interest effect will multiply your money over the years.

If you are late in your career and saving regularly, I would challenge you to ask yourself if you can save more, because realistically, the alternative is working longer.

This is your retirement! The only person that can help or hinder your dreams of living overseas during that time period is you. Consider saving additional money in a traditional or Roth IRA. The tax treatment of the two types of accounts vary and the implications can be significant. The maximum contribution limit is $5,500 a year. If you are 50 years old or older, you can contribute an additional $1,000 that could be useful in helping you reach your goal.

Lastly, know the specifics of your social security benefits. You remember those social security taxes that came out of Joe's paycheck? Well, as you work, you are paying into a social security system that is meant to pay you back when you retire. Using the Social Security Administration's online resources or speaking with an advisor can help you estimate your social security benefit better.

I stress retirement planning heavily because the battle against inflation is a challenging one. If you don't save and properly invest a portion of your earnings earmarked for retirement, you will without a doubt lose the fight. Every day, the goods and services that you purchase get more and more expensive. Inflation was described by investment guru Benjamin Graham in his book, *The Intel-*

ligent Investor: The Definitive Book on Value Investing, with one simple line. He says, "In the 1950s, it took two adults to carry $20 worth of groceries. Today, it takes a five-year-old." Inflation is the general increase in prices and the fall of the purchasing power of money. It is imperative that you plan for retirement because today's dollars without interest will not be able to furnish tomorrow's needs.

Investments

There are several types of investments that an individual can make. The problem is that people oftentimes only seek riches without a defined goal in place. In these circumstances, a person is willing to take on any amount of risk and may make emotional investment decisions for which there is no plan of action, no reason for why they are investing, they just want to make money. Bad deal.

The better approach towards making an investment is to start with an investment objective. The investment objective poses all the *why* questions and extracts pertinent data that may help a financial professional provide the best vehicles to help you reach your short- and long-term goals. An individual typically doesn't disclose this information until they are certain that they will work with a specific advisor.

The investment objective typically comes in the form of a questionnaire, or the information can be discovered through an interview-like conversation with your chosen advisor. The conversation should include both qualitative and quantitative characteristics of the person or family that seeks to reach a specific goal. Qualitative measures that should be covered are your risk tolerance, investment time horizon and restrictions on any investments such as sin stocks (tobacco and liquor companies, etc.) Quantitative characteristics that should be discussed are your personal net worth, liquid net worth outlining the cash you have available today, retirement and investment account balances, income and expense levels. Only after this information is documented can an advisor match the vehicles necessary for you to reach your goals.

Time horizon is an important factor to consider when planning for investments. Time horizon measures the amount of time before an investment has to be liquated for use for a specific goal. As markets are cyclical in nature, the more time you have, the more aggressive you can be with your investments because you have time to recover for any losses that you may incur. The lesser the amount of time available, the less risk you can take, and if you are not on track to your goals, that means your savings and contribution amounts will have to be significantly higher. Outlining your time horizon for a financial professional is extremely important when choosing the appropriate risk tolerance and asset allocation of your portfolio.

Do you remember the television game show, *Who Wants To Be A Millionaire?* The famous episode of John Carpenter, the show's first ever one millionaire dollar prize winner, described to us exactly what risk tolerance is. As Carpenter looked across his monitor into the eyes of Regis Philbin, you could tell that his blood pressure had not risen one bit. In fact, for the entire segment, he did not break a sweat from any of the questions that he was asked.

It was the moment of truth. Carpenter found himself one question away from being the first contestant to win the grand prize of one million dollars. As the lights dimmed and focused on Carpenter and Philbin, you could feel the suspense from your television screen. Carpenter had all of his lifelines and was seemingly unbothered by the implications of this single question. His demeanor came as much of a surprise for Philbin as well.

To remind him of what was at stake, Regis explained that if he should miss this question he'll be reduced from $500,000 in winnings to $32,000. Regis then proceeded to ask the million-dollar question. "Which of these U.S. Presidents appeared on the television series *Laugh-In*?" With a smirk and a chuckle, Carpenter opted to finally use one of his lifelines to call his parents. Instead of asking for help from a trusted friend, he confidently told his father that he was going to win the million dollars. And shortly after, he did.

In 19 minutes, Carpenter taught us a lesson about risk tolerance, a fundamental concept when investing assets for future growth. By definition, risk tolerance is the degree of variability in investment returns that an individual is willing to withstand. For many of us, we understand risk tolerance as "high risk, high reward." The old age expectation of investing is that when you put your money in an account, over time, this principal will grow to a desired dollar amount that will help you achieve your goals in the future. What risk tolerance considers is exactly how your money will grow by the variance or fluctuation of the assets during up and down markets and what pitfalls are to be expected along the way.

Let's take John Carpenter, for example. Carpenter had already secured $500,000 in winnings from the game show. If he were to leave the show at this time, he would've left a richer man than when he had entered. In assessing his risk tolerance (and knowledge), he knew that he was comfortable with a dramatic loss in principle, which could have potentially left him with $32,000 if he had answered the question incorrectly. Now, if you were Carpenter on the game show, or even with your current portfolio, what would you have done? Would you have taken $500,000, or would you have risked losing $468,000 on one question?

Even though historical data shows that with time and an investment plan, there's a favorable likelihood that with discipline you'll reach your goals, the risk tolerance question still applies to exactly how you want to reach them. Carpenter's confidence in his knowledge and risk tolerance gave him an "aggressive" investor money personality. He knew what his goal was, what fluctuations he could stomach, and he took the necessary risk to achieve his goal. Your task, with the help of your financial advisor, is to figure out what risk you can stomach to achieve your reward.

There's a reason why you may feel comfortable with all of your money in a savings account or in a low yielding CD, and quite honestly, there is nothing wrong with those vehicles. In the right circumstance, they certainly have their place in a financial plan, but how do they help you reach your goals? You can't expect Ferrari speed with minivan risk, but the later you wait to invest, a minivan may be all you can afford.

Asset allocation is the last piece to get familiar with. You'll work with your relationship coaches on this, but be familiar with the term. Asset allocation is simply a general investment strategy that an advisor uses to build out your investment portfolio. You can think of asset allocation as the ingredients to a recipe. When baking a cake, you may be asked to use a certain amount of sugar and flour. What they won't tell you is exactly what brand of sugar to buy, as long as it gets the job done.

Your advisor will outline the general portions of stocks, bonds and other investment vehicles that will make up your investment portfolio. This allocation could change over time as you edge closer towards your goals or change your risk tolerance, but it is used as a way for your advisors to stay disciplined, track the performance of individual investments and set proper expectations.

The term *diversification* is a familiar one when it comes to investing. Everyone knows that you have to diversify your portfolio, but not everyone knows exactly what it means and why it is important. Diversification is a risk management strategy that mixes a variety of investment options within your portfolio to reduce the amount of risk on your overall portfolio. This technique attempts to avoid and reduce the losses of your principal because of the poor performance of a single investment choice. Most people understand the theory of diversification as not putting all of your eggs in one basket.

You can view diversification as a four-lane highway. In the far left or fast lane, you have your aggressive investments that are going five to ten miles over the speed limit. In the middle lanes you have your more moderate investments that are doing the speed limit, and in the slow lane are the investments that are more conservative and slower moving. Your risk tolerance will dictate the weighting of your assets between these categories. Diversification is important because like a traffic jam, different lanes on the speedway begin to have an advantage. As economic events happen, more conservative investments may lead the charge. In times of economic growth, the "fast lane" investments may lead the pack. Knowing the basics of these concepts will help you understand the plans that your advisor sets forth for you.

Insurance

Insurance is something that people have a love-hate relationship with. On one hand, when an unfortunate event occurs, they love to know that they are covered by insurance, whether its property, auto, life or health. On the other hand, some people hate dealing with those pesky insurance agents who want to sell them more coverage than they think they actually need. I agree, some insurance agents are completely outlandish with their projections, as they don't consider your circumstances and what you can actually afford. But, you wouldn't challenge a trusted doctor with his diagnosis, would you?

For the purposes of this book, we'll talk only about life and health insurance. Everyone needs to have it and there are no exceptions. Life insurance is important because it protects the wealth and assets that you have already built, accommodates your family for burial arrangements and can help your family maintain their standard of living.

The proper course of action is an insurance needs analysis. The needs analysis answers the question of the amount of insurance you need, then takes into consideration how much you can afford. The insurance needs analysis will take into consideration how much income your family would need if, God forbid, you were to pass away today. It will assess how many years the income will be provided and any additional income sources that you currently receive.

The analysis then dives into your personal net worth, particularly your expenses and your debt. Generally, this includes mortgage debt, desired funds that will go toward your children's college education and other debt. This section of your analysis will factor in final expenses for your burial as well. Lastly, it will estimate the amount of savings and investments that you have accumulated over the years, including any existing life insurance that you may have. With this information, your financial professional, along with his team of underwriters, will prepare and estimate that will take care of your family in your absence.

There's no easy way to talk about life insurance, but

everyone needs to have the discussion. The primary benefits of life insurance are to protect your loved ones, to leave a legacy, pay off debts and expenses and to increase financial security. Alternatively, some life insurance vehicles can be used as a vehicle for tax efficiency and additional savings. Speaking to a professional about your options would be best to assess your individual needs.

Taxes

The tax part of the process is where you really need the assistance of a tax professional. Taxes are tricky and not easy to understand. In terms of their correlation to investments and growing your wealth, there are investment vehicles such as the traditional IRA that can help reduce your tax liability come tax season if you fall within designated income limits.

Some additional things to consider are your current income brackets, implications of self-employment, filing status, exemptions and inclusions. If you are currently living in retirement, understanding the taxation of your retirement assets and social security benefits is highly important. Consider all deductions, both standard and itemized, that can help reduce your tax liabilities. The IRS website can be a good resource for what things should be considered.

Rule of one-third

For those that receive a tax return, there's a strategy that I recommend you utilize to maximize your return. This strategy is called the rule of one-third. I know that life has its ups and downs and that saving every penny that you earn is virtually impossible to do. We are only human. The rule of one-third suggests that upon receiving your tax return, you earmark the funds for three specific things: debt, personal need and an investment.

Using this strategy, you'll contribute one-third of your tax returns toward outstanding debt such as a consumer credit card or loan. You'll then contribute one-third of the assets to a right-now need. Maybe you have a portion of your house that needs to be fixed or you need to purchase something for yourself. Whatever the case may be, this portion of the return should be used on you. The final third of the money should be contributed to an investment account. Even if the amount isn't that large, if we stick to the time value of money principle, we know that the amount will be worth more at a future date. The rule of one-third is a general guideline for what to do with your tax returns. Depending on your individual circumstance, you can shift the percentage contribution between the three categories.

Good investment advisors work hand-in-hand with tax professionals to make sure that your strategies align and that you are saving as much money as possible in taxes. Speaking to a licensed tax professional on this subject would be a great starting point on understanding the basics about your tax situation.

Estate planning

Like the conversation of life insurance, estate planning can be a touchy subject for many people, but from my experience, having the conversation and setting up estate plans when necessary helps families with the division and taxation of assets after the passing of a loved one. There are benefits to having an estate plan, the first being that you have control of all of your assets while you are alive, regardless of your financial circumstance, age or health condition. Secondly, an estate plan protects you and your loved ones from unnecessary probate taxes, court costs, professional fees and state and, in some cases, "death" taxes.

One key benefit is that a properly drafted and well-executed estate plan can provide instructions on how you want to take care of yourself and your family in the event of death or a disability. The estate plan will ensure that you designate who gets what, when they get it and in the way you want them to receive it.

Typically, a starting point for the estate plan is the beneficiary designation on you investment accounts. The beneficiary listed will be the person(s) that will be eligible to receive the distributions from your accounts, trust and will or life insurance policy. The preferred route is to name beneficiaries on your accounts and estate planning documents, but the court can also appoint them.

Remember, an estate plan should be seen as a balance of the taxation of assets and provide for your loved one. Through my experience, individuals that focus on the people that they love find much more peace of mind in the stipulations of their estate plan. You should work closely with an estate attorney to figure out the best options for your estate planning needs.

Emergency fund

Generally, the "E" in the RIIITE Planning Process stands for estate planning, but I recognize that everyone isn't prepared nor at the point where estate planning is one of their top priorities. In this day and age where millennials and professionals are planning earlier, an area that often gets overlooked is the emergency fund. An emergency fund is an account used to set aside cash for an unexpected event. These events include an unexpected illness, loss of job and major personal expenses. The fund serves as a safety net for your financial plan and helps to not disrupt the accumulation of wealth that is taking place in your investment accounts. The emergency fund is great for additional financial security and helps reduce the use of the dating downfall of credit cards and other consumer credit options.

As I sit across from clients and prospects, the questions of "how much is enough?" and "which assets should be kept in this fund?" always arise. Mainstream financial coaches suggest 3 to 6 months of total expenses. That is a good range, but there is a bit of detail to the rule. First, before any advisor can prescribe, he first has to diagnose. Your individual situation has to be taken into consideration before deciding how much money should be in your emergency fund.

Three months' worth of income should be considered if the client is married and both spouses are employed, or if the client is married, but only one spouse is employed and there is a second source of income available to the family. The last circumstance that would warrant an emergency fund worth three months' worth of a total of your fixed and variable expenses would be if you are single with a considerable second source of income such as alimony payments, an inheritance or a trust fund. The six-month emergency fund should be considered when the client is a single wage earner or if only one spouse is employed.

A major point to remember for the emergency fund is that it should be kept in easily accessible, liquid assets. Many people are rich on paper, but they find themselves in a jam when they can't sell one of their properties that they own. Because of this, the best course of action is to accumulate the money for your emergency fund inside of a savings account, money market deposit accounts, or a checking account. As life has its ebbs and flows, make sure that you prepare for the good and bad days.

Questions That Need Answers

1. What is your priority out of retirement, investments, insurance, tax and estate planning?

_____

_____

_____

_____

_____

2. If you were in John Carpenter's situation, would you have taken the money, or risked $468,000 on one question?

_____

_____

_____

_____

_____

3. Do you pay or receive taxes? If you have a tax bill, what have you done to reduce your tax liability? If you receive a return, how have you used it in the past?

_____

_____

_____

_____

_____

_____

4. Are you putting all of your eggs in one basket?

_____

_____

_____

_____

_____

_____

5. Do you have an adequate emergency fund? Why or why not? Are your assets liquid?

_____

_____

_____

_____

_____

_____

6. Do you have insurance coverage? Are you certain that it is enough?

_____

_____

_____

_____

_____

_____

7. Have you designated beneficiaries on your investment accounts?

_____

_____

_____

_____

_____

_____

Part 4: Finding Your Relationship Coaches

"If it weren't for my coaches, we would've lost the game before it started."

In your relationship with Benji, financial advisors, accountants and estate planning attorneys are pivotal in helping individuals reach their investment goals. This section is intended to give you direction on how to find your relationship coaches.

Finding a Financial Advisor: How to Spot a Wolf in Sheep's Clothes

Ah. There he is, your financial advisor, Steve.

Do you remember when you met Steve? I do. It was a phone call that you received one evening after work when Steve told you about the fantastic products that he has that could help you diversify your portfolio. You're older, have made career advancements over the years and you think to yourself, *it's really about time for me to start taking my personal financial planning seriously.*

Instead of politely hanging up, you decided to hear him out. Steve let you know how investors are fearful of the current state of the market, how his brokerage is a bit different than your current advisors' and how his products are unparalleled. He touched on every emotion that you'd been feeling for quite some time. So you agreed to meet.

Below are some ways to identify a wolf in sheep's clothes:

- ***The advisor is not a fiduciary.*** If an advisor is a fiduciary, he or she has a legal obligation to put your interests first. According to the 1830 Prudent Person Standard of Care, the advisor that acts as a fiduciary must act with the needs of the beneficiary in mind. While this cannot guarantee good conduct on behalf the advisor, it provides a hard guideline for the advisor and an expectation for his clients.

- ***The advisor holds custody of assets.*** If you're writing a check to your advisor, you may want to pump the brakes. Financial fraud can occur when people write checks to their advisors or the firms that they own. Think Bernie Madoff.

- ***The advisor leads with commission-based products.*** You've just sat with Steve for hours. You tell him how you want to retire early, have your mortgage paid off at retirement and travel the world with the love of your life. Steve's response? You need life insurance!

A true advisor will diagnose before he prescribes and will make appropriate recommendations, even if it doesn't yield him the biggest monetary benefit. This is the sign of a true fiduciary.

- ***The advisor doesn't speak of a plan or strategy.*** Benjamin Franklin once said, "Failing to prepare is preparing to fail." Your advisor should outline his strategy for the investment of your assets and/or a plan to help you reach your investment objectives.

- ***The advisor dances around fees.*** It is my hope that you have a good relationship with your advisor. If so, you understand that your advisor needs to be paid for his expertise. Great! But, your advisor still has the responsibility of being transparent with you on the subject of fees. Is he paid a salary from his employer? Is she on a split salary and commission schedule? Are they fee-based or fee-only? Or is it a pure commission schedule? Understanding how your advisor is compensated could help you foresee the type of advice that you'll receive. If he needs to make a sale to keep the lights on, it's unlikely that he's thinking about your long-term objectives.

- ***The advisor uses expensive investments.*** As the saying goes, a dollar saved is a dollar earned. Your hard-earned money should not fall victim to expensive mutual fund fees, high annuity maintenance fees, pricey proprietary products and above average commissions on stock trades.

  The advisor should use cost-effective mutual funds, exchange-traded funds, no-load funds and a firm that has reasonable trade commissions. More expensive investment vehicles may be necessary depending on individual needs. Essentially, the advisor should do everything within their power to keep more money in your pocket.

- ***The advisor isn't around when needed.*** Like in any relationship, it's very easy to be around when things are good. The mark of a great advisor is how close he is to you when things aren't so good. When the market is down or choppy, do you receive an email or call? Does he call you periodically to do a temperature check? Actions speak much louder than words and can provide clear signs of a wolf.

Financial planning is something that everyone will have to consider at some point in their lives, and picking the right advisor can literally pay dividends in the future. Be sure to choose an advisor that you like, that you trust, and that can issue advice with you in mind.

Points to Remember with Do-It-Yourselfers in Mind

Let me start by saying that there's nothing wrong with fitting this profile. Do you remember the time when you tried to change your own oil? The t-shirt you wore had to be disposed of. Or the time you decided to assemble all of the chairs in the living room once they arrived from the store? They're still a little wobbly, but no one has hurt themselves yet. How about the time... Okay, I'll stop.

It hasn't all been bad. In fact, you've done a few successful things: painted your child's room with your spouse, organized the closet to maximize the space and put your spare on when you had a flat tire. You see, as a do-it-yourselfer, you are always up for a new exhibition and eager to be challenged. You find satisfaction in achieving unique tasks that open the door for great conversation.

With today's technology, everyone thinks that they can manage their own assets and not get their emotions involved. No problem! Right? Wrong. While there are many individuals who enjoy researching capital markets and are very successful at investing their personal assets themselves, having a professional on your side is not a bad idea.

Below are a few points to remember with do-it-your-selfers in mind:

- **An advisor can be your sounding board.** There's nothing wrong with being a do-it-your-selfer. If you have enough time and are truly up for the challenge, it can work for you. The best do-it-yourselfers employ an advisor to bounce investment ideas off of. After all, the advisor can help offer a perspective that you may not have considered in your own research efforts.

- **Serious money should be separate from hobby dollars.** The truth is most do-it-your-selfers know that investing isn't a career for them. Typically, they have careers, are very smart and are indeed capable of getting the job done. But, investing your hard-earned money deserves more than just hobby time.

If you feel like you'd be interested in dabbling in investing as a hobby, use a capable financial advisor to manage the money that you can't afford to lose. You'll thank yourself in the long run.

- **Robo-advisors can't calculate your concerns.** Technology has evolved by leaps and bounds over the last few decades. We even have cars that can drive themselves! It's not a surprise that there are platforms that allow robots to handle *all* of your investment concerns.

  Do you worry when the market is volatile? How about when you'd like to know how the presidential election will affect your portfolio? While there are situations in which a robo-investing platform may be a good fit, a human may be a better fit for your individual needs and concerns.

- **Where's the plan?** Do-it-yourself investing can perpetuate investing based on fear and greed, which can weaken overall investment returns and lead to taking unnecessary risks. People tend to sell during financial lows, and buy as prices increase—losing a lot of money over the long term. An advisor can help you implement a plan, help to mitigate risk and prevent you from making costly investment decisions.

- **Don't overlook Uncle Sam.** Buy here, sell there. Maybe you'll try options tomorrow? The buying and selling of securities may create taxable events now or in the future. Taxes are very complicated. The do-it-yourself investor may not know all of the tax consequences behind the decisions that they make within their investment portfolios. These are just a few things to consider when taking on the responsibility of managing your own investments. A financial advisor that can provide advice with you in mind can be the difference between reaching your goals and falling short.

Part 5: From Me to You

As a youth, I was told that once you have the tools to do better, you have a decision to make. *Dating Benji: Straight Talk on Improving Your Relationship with Money* gives you the tools to be the best that you can be in your relationship with your personal finances. It takes you through some of the reasons why you may have failed and has asks you pivotal questions on why exactly you have had pitfalls in your journey towards your money goals. I must admit that financial planning is not an easy task. It seems impossible to stretch the funds that we have towards all of the demands of the RIITE Planning Process and the basic necessities of life. Not to mention, life is meant to be lived. I understand.

Dating Benji is my gift to you. Let it serve as an instrument for your money tool box. If you consider all of the things learned, follow the RIITE Planning Process and find trustworthy financial professionals to walk along aside you on your journey, success is waiting for you at the end of the road. May you and Benji live happily ever after.

Glossary

1035 EXCHANGE

A method of exchanging insurance-related assets without triggering a taxable event. Cash-value life insurance policies and annuity contracts are two products that may qualify for a 1035 exchange.

401(K) PLAN

A qualified retirement plan available to eligible employees of companies. 401(k) plans allow eligible employees to defer taxation on a specific percentage of their income that is to be put toward retirement savings; taxes on this deferred income and on any earnings the account generates are deferred until the funds are withdrawn—normally in retirement. Employers may match part or all of an employee's contributions. Employees may be responsible for investment selections and enjoy the direct tax savings.

401(K) LOAN

A loan taken from the assets within a 401(k) account. 401(k) loans charge interest and are normally paid back through payroll deductions. If the borrower leaves an employer before a 401(k) loan has been repaid, the full amount of the loan is generally due. If the borrower fails to repay the loan, it is considered a distribution, and ordinary income taxes may be due, along with any applicable tax penalties.

403(B) PLAN

A 403(b) plan is similar to a 401(k). A 403(b) is a qualified retirement plan available to employees of non-profit and government organizations.

Account Balance

The amount held in an account at the end of a reporting period. For example, a credit card account balance would show the amount owed to a lender as a result of purchases made during a specific period.

ADJUSTABLE-RATE MORTGAGE (ARM)

A mortgage with an interest rate that is adjusted periodically based on an index. Adjustable-rate mortgages generally have lower initial interest rates than fixed-rate mortgages because the lender is able to transfer some of the risk to the borrower; if prevailing rates go higher, the interest rate on a variable mortgage may adjust upward as well.

ADJUSTED GROSS INCOME (AGI)

One figure used in the calculation of income tax liability. AGI is determined by subtracting allowable adjustments from gross income.

ADMINISTRATOR

A probate-court-appointed person who is tasked with settling an estate for which there is no will.

AFTER-TAX RETURN

The return on an investment after subtracting any taxes due.

AGGRESSIVE GROWTH FUND

A mutual fund offered by an investment company that specifically pursues substantial capital gains. Mutual fund balances are subject to fluctuation in value and market risk. Shares, when redeemed, may be worth more or less than their original cost. Mutual funds are sold only by prospectus. Individuals are encouraged to consider the charges, risks, expenses, and investment objectives carefully before investing. A prospectus containing this and other information about the investment company can be obtained from your financial professional. Read it carefully before you invest or send money.

ALTERNATIVE MINIMUM TAX (AMT)

A method of calculating income tax with a unique set of rules for deductions and exemptions that are more restrictive than those in the traditional tax system. The AMT attempts to ensure that certain high-income taxpayers don't pay a lower effective tax rate than everyone else. To determine whether or not the AMT applies, taxpayers must fill out IRS Form 6251.

AMERICAN STOCK EXCHANGE (AMEX)

A stock exchange originally located in New York City. AMEX was taken over by NYSE Euronext—the group that operates the New York Stock Exchange—in January 2009.

ANNUAL PERCENTAGE RATE (APR)

The yearly cost of a loan expressed as a percentage of the loan amount. The APR includes interest owed and any fees or additional costs associated with the agreement.

ANNUAL REPORT

A report required by the Securities and Exchange Commission (SEC) of any company issuing registered stock, that describes a company's management, operations, and financial reports. Annual reports are sent to shareholders, and must also be available for public review.

ANNUITY

A contract with an insurance company that guarantees current or future payments in exchange for a premium or series of premiums. The interest earned on an annuity contract is not taxable until the funds are paid out or withdrawn. Withdrawals and income payments are taxed as ordinary income. If a withdrawal is made prior to age 59½, penalties may apply. The guarantees of an annuity contract depend on the issuing company's claims-paying ability. Annuities have fees and charges associated with the contract, and a surrender charge also may apply if the contract owner elects to give up the annuity before certain time-period conditions are satisfied.

APPRAISAL

A formal assessment of a property's value at a specific point in time, performed by a qualified professional.

ASSET

Anything owned that has a current value that may provide a future benefit.

ASSET ALLOCATION

A method of allocating funds to pursue the highest potential return at a specific level of risk. Asset allocation normally uses sophisticated mathematical analysis of the historical performance of asset classes to attempt to project future risk and return. Asset allocation is an approach to help manage investment risk. It does not guarantee against investment loss.

ASSET CLASS

A specific category of investments that share similar characteristics and tend to behave similarly in the marketplace.

AUDIT

In accounting, the formal examination of a company's financial records by a qualified professional to determine the records' accuracy, consistency, and conformity to legal standards and established accounting principles. In taxes, the formal examination of a tax return by the Internal Revenue Service or other authority to determine its accuracy.

AUTOMATIC REINVESTMENT

An arrangement under which an institution automatically deposits dividends or capital gains generated by an individual's investment back into the investment to purchase additional shares.

Balanced Mutual Fund

A mutual fund offered by an investment company which attempts to hold a balance of stocks and bonds. Mutual funds are subject to fluctuation in value and market risk. Shares, when redeemed, may be worth more or less than their original cost. Mutual funds are sold only by prospectus. Individuals are encouraged to consider the charges, risks, expenses, and investment objectives carefully before investing. A prospectus containing this and other information about the investment company can be obtained from your financial professional. Read it carefully before you invest or send money.

BEAR MARKET

A market experiencing an extended period of declining prices. A bear market is the opposite of a bull market.

BENEFICIARY

The person or entity who will receive benefits from a life insurance policy, qualified retirement plan, annuity, trust, or will upon the death of an individual.

BLUE CHIP STOCK

The stock of an established company which has a history of generating a profit and possibly a consistent dividend.

BOND

A debt instrument under which the issuer promises to pay a specified amount of interest and to repay the principal at maturity. The market value of a bond will fluctuate with changes in interest rates. As rates rise, the value of existing bonds typically falls. If an investor sells a bond before maturity, it may be worth more or less than the initial purchase price. By holding a bond to maturity, an investor will receive the interest payments due plus his or her original principal, barring default by the issuer. Investments seeking to achieve higher yields also involve a higher degree of risk.

BOOK VALUE

The value of a company's assets minus its liabilities, preferred stock, and redeemable preferred stock.

BULL MARKET

A market experiencing an extended period of rising prices. A bull market is the opposite of a bear market.

BUY-AND-HOLD

An investment strategy that advocates holding securities for the long term and ignoring short-term price fluctuations in the market.

BUY-SELL AGREEMENT

A legal contract that provides for the purchase of all outstanding shares from a business owner who wishes to sell, wants to terminate involvement, is permanently disabled, or has died. Buy-sell agreements are often funded with life insurance.

CAPITAL GAIN OR LOSS

The difference between the price at which an asset was purchased and the price for which it was sold. When the sale price is higher than the purchase price, the difference is a capital gain; when the sale price is lower than the purchase price, the difference is a capital loss.

CASH ALTERNATIVES

Assets that are most easily converted into cash and which have a very low risk of price fluctuation. For example, money market funds may be considered a cash alternative. Money held in money market funds is not insured or guaranteed by the Federal Deposit Insurance Corporation or any other government agency. Money market funds seek to preserve the value of your investment at $1.00 a share. However, it is possible to lose money by investing in a money market fund.

CASH SURRENDER VALUE

The amount a policyholder would receive when voluntarily terminating a cash-value life insurance policy before the insured event occurs or when cashing out an annuity contract before its maturity. Computation of cash surrender value is stated in the life insurance or annuity contract.

CERTIFICATE OF DEPOSIT (CD)

A deposit with a bank, thrift institution, or credit union that promises a fixed interest rate on funds deposited for a specified period of time. Bank savings accounts and CDs are FDIC insured up to $250,000 per depositor per institution and generally provide a fixed rate of return, whereas the value of money market mutual funds can fluctuate.

CHARITABLE LEAD TRUST

A trust established for the benefit of a charitable organization under which the charitable organization receives payment of a specified amount (at least annually) from the trust. On the death of the grantor, remainder interest in the trust passes to his or her heirs. Using a trust involves a complex set of tax rules and regulations. Before moving forward with a trust, consider working with a professional who is familiar with the rules and regulations.

CHARITABLE REMAINDER TRUST

A trust established for the benefit of a charitable organization under which the grantor can designate an income beneficiary to receive payment of a specified amount—at least annually—from the trust. The grantor may also be the income beneficiary. On the death of the grantor, remainder interest in the trust passes to the charitable organization. Using a trust involves a complex set of tax rules and regulations. Before moving forward with a trust, consider working with a professional who is familiar with the rules and regulations.

CLAIM

A request for payment under the terms of an insurance policy.

COBRA

A federal law that requires group health plans sponsored by employers with more than 20 employees to offer terminated or retired employees the opportunity to continue their health insurance coverage for a specified period at the employees' expense.

COINSURANCE OR CO-PAYMENT

A policy provision under which an insurance company and the insured party share the total cost of covered medical services after the policy's deductible has been met.

COMMERCIAL PAPER

An unsecured, short-term debt security issued by a corporation to finance short-term liabilities. These notes are normally backed only by the issuing corporation's promise to pay the face amount on the maturity date specified on the note, which is usually less than six months.

COMMON STOCK

A security that represents partial ownership of a corporation. Those who hold common stock are entitled to participate in stockholder meetings, to vote for the board of directors, and may receive periodic dividends.

COMMUNITY PROPERTY

State laws under which most property and debts acquired during a marriage—except for gifts or inheritances—are owned jointly by both spouses and are divided upon divorce or annulment. In the United States, nine states have community property laws: Arizona, California, Idaho, Louisiana, Nevada, New Mexico, Texas, Washington, and Wisconsin.

COMPOUND INTEREST

A process under which interest is computed both on an account's principal and on any gains reinvested in prior periods. This is contrasted with simple interest, in which interest is calculated only on the principal amount.

CONSUMER PRICE INDEX (CPI)

The U.S. government's main measure of inflation, calculated monthly by the Department of Labor.

CONVERTIBLE TERM INSURANCE

A term life insurance policy under which the policyholder has the right to convert the policy to permanent life insurance, subject to limitations. Several factors will affect the cost and availability of life insurance, including age, health, and the type and amount of insurance purchased. Life insurance policies have expenses, including mortality and other charges. You should consider determining whether you are insurable before implementing a strategy involving life insurance. Any guarantees associated with a policy are dependent on the ability of the issuing insurance company to continue making claim payments.

CORPORATE BOND

A debt security issued by a corporation under which the issuer promises to make periodic interest payments and to repay the investor's principal at maturity. The market value of a bond will fluctuate with changes in interest rates. As rates rise, the value of existing bonds typically falls. If an investor sells a bond before maturity, it may be worth more or less than the initial purchase price. By holding a bond to maturity, investors will receive the interest payments due plus their original principal, barring default by the issuer. Investments seeking to achieve higher yields also involve a higher degree of risk.

CORPORATION

A legal organization created under the laws of a state as a separate legal entity that has privileges and liabilities that are distinct from those of its members. Corporations are taxable entities—they are taxed separately from their members or shareholders. Corporations are able to borrow money and to make a profit separately from their members or shareholders.

COVERDELL EDUCATION SAVINGS ACCOUNT (COVERDELL ESA)

A tax-advantaged investment account that allows accumulation of funds to cover future education expenses, subject to limitations. Coverdell ESAs allow money to grow tax deferred and proceeds to be withdrawn tax free for qualified education expenses at a qualified institution.

CREDIT SCORE

A statistical estimation of how likely a potential borrower is to pay his or her debts and, by extension, how much credit he or she should have.

Debt

An obligation owed by one party (the debtor) to a second party (the creditor).

DEBT-TO-EQUITY RATIO

The ratio of a company's total debt to its total shareholder equity. Some use the debt-to-equity ratio to attempt to ascertain a company's capability to repay its creditors.

DEDUCTION

An amount that can be subtracted from gross income before income taxes are calculated.

DEED

A legal document that confirms ownership of an asset or that confirms the passage of an interest, right, or ownership in the asset from one person or legal entity to another.

DEFERRED ANNUITY

A contract with an insurance company that guarantees a future payment or series of payments in exchange for current premiums. The interest earned on an annuity contract is not taxable until the funds are paid out or withdrawn. The guarantees of an annuity contract depend on the issuing company's claims-paying ability. Annuities have fees and charges associated with the contract, and a surrender charge also may apply if the contract owner elects to give up the annuity before certain time-period conditions are satisfied.

DEFINED BENEFIT PLAN

A retirement plan under which the benefit to a retiring employee is defined. Defined benefit plans are normally funded by employer contributions.

DEFINED CONTRIBUTION PLAN

A retirement plan under which the annual contributions made by the employer or employee are defined. Benefits may vary depending on the performance of the investments in the account.

DEFLATION

A reduction in the price of goods and services. Deflation is the opposite of inflation.

DEPENDENT

A person who relies on another for his or her financial support. Within limits, those who support dependents are allowed to claim certain exemptions when filing income taxes.

DIRECT ROLLOVER

The direct transfer of assets from the trustee or custodian of one qualified retirement plan or account to the trustee or custodian of another. Done correctly, direct rollovers do not trigger taxable events.

DISABILITY INCOME INSURANCE

An insurance policy that pays a portion of the insured's income when a specified disability makes working uncomfortable, painful, or impossible.

DIVERSIFICATION

An investment strategy under which capital is divided among several assets or asset classes. Diversification operates under the assumption that different assets and/or asset classes are unlikely to move in the same direction, allowing gains in one investment to offset losses in another. Diversification is an approach to help manage investment risk. It does not eliminate the risk of loss if security prices decline.

DIVIDEND

Taxable payments made by a company to its shareholders. Some dividends are paid quarterly and others are paid monthly. Companies can adjust common share dividends at any time, pending approval by the company's board of directors.

DOLLAR-COST AVERAGING

An investment strategy under which a fixed dollar amount of securities is purchased at regular intervals. Under dollar-cost averaging, more shares are purchased when prices are low and fewer shares when prices rise. Keep in mind that dollar-cost averaging does not protect against a loss in a declining market or guarantee a profit in a rising market. Investors should evaluate their financial ability to continue making purchases through periods of declining and rising prices.

DOW JONES INDUSTRIAL AVERAGE (DJIA)

An average calculated by summing the prices of 30 actively leading stocks on the New York Stock Exchange (NYSE) and dividing the sum by a divisor which has been adjusted to account for cases of stock splits, spinoffs, or similar structural changes. Individuals cannot invest directly in an index.

EARLY WITHDRAWAL

Withdrawal of funds from an investment before its maturity date or withdrawal of funds from a tax-deferred account before the legally imposed age requirements have been satisfied. Early withdrawals may be subject to penalties.

EMPLOYEE STOCK OWNERSHIP PLAN (ESOP)

A defined-contribution plan that provides a company's workers with an ownership interest in the company—usually as shares of company stock.

EMPLOYER-SPONSORED RETIREMENT PLAN

A retirement plan sponsored by an employer for the benefit of its employees. These typically fall into one of two types: defined-contribution plans (such as SEP IRAs, 401(k) plans and 403(b) plans) and defined-benefit plans (such as traditional pensions).

EQUITY

The value of real property or a business after all liabilities have been paid. A home worth $300,000 with a $200,000 mortgage would have $100,000 in equity.

EMPLOYEE RETIREMENT INCOME SECURITY ACT (ERISA)

A federal law that establishes the regulations under which retirement plans are governed and spells out the federal income tax regulations and effects for qualified retirement plans.

ESTATE MANAGEMENT

The preparations necessary to manage a person's financial and healthcare matters during his or her lifetime and to effectively and economically distribute the assets within that estate upon his or her death.

ESTATE TAX

Federal and/or state taxes that may be levied on the assets of a deceased person upon his or her death. These taxes are paid by the deceased person's estate rather than his or her heirs.

EXCHANGE-TRADED FUNDS (ETFS)

A share of an investment company that owns a block of shares selected to pursue a specific investment objective. ETFs trade like stocks and are listed on stock exchanges and sold by broker-dealers. Exchange-traded funds are sold only by prospectus. Please consider the charges, risks, expenses, and investment objectives carefully before investing. A prospectus containing this and other information about the investment company can be obtained from your financial professional. Read it carefully before you invest or send money.

EXECUTIVE BONUS PLAN

An executive benefit paid for by an employer.

EXECUTOR

A person named by a will or appointed by the probate court to distribute the deceased's assets as directed by the will or, in the absence of a will, in accordance with the probate laws of the state.

FEDERAL INCOME TAX BRACKET

A series of income ranges within which a taxpayer's income is taxed at a certain rate. Taxpayers pay the tax rate in a given bracket only for that portion of their overall income that falls within the bracket's range.

FEDERAL RESERVE SYSTEM (THE FED)

The United States' central bank. The Federal Reserve System consists of a series of 12 independent banks that operate under the supervision of a seven-member, federally appointed board of governors. The Fed strives to maintain maximum employment, stable price levels, and moderate long-term interest rates. It establishes and enforces the regulations banks, savings and loans, and credit unions must follow. It also acts as a clearing house for certain financial transactions and provides banking services to the federal government.

FINANCIAL AID

Loans, grants, scholarships, and work-study programs provided by federally and privately funded sources to enable students to attend college.

FINANCIAL STATEMENT

A formal record of the financial activities of a business, person, or other entity. For a business, financial statements typically include a balance sheet, a profit and loss statement, and a cash flow statement.

FINANCIAL INDUSTRY REGULATORY AUTHORITY (FINRA)

FINRA is an independent regulator that oversees all securities firms doing business in the U.S. FINRA seeks to protect investors by making sure the securities industry operates fairly and honestly.

FIRST-TO-DIE LIFE INSURANCE

Joint life insurance taken out on the lives of two or more people that pays its death benefit when the first insured person dies.

FIXED ANNUITY

A contract with an insurance company that guarantees investment growth at a fixed interest rate as well as current or future payments in exchange for a premium or series of premiums. The interest earned on an annuity contract is not taxable until the funds are paid out or withdrawn. The guarantees of an annuity contract depend on the issuing company's claims-paying ability. Annuities have fees and charges associated with the contract, and a surrender charge also may apply if the contract owner elects to give up the annuity before certain time-period conditions are satisfied.

FIXED-RATE MORTGAGE

A mortgage with a set interest rate that will not change over the life of the loan.

FORECLOSURE

The legal process under which a creditor seizes the property of a borrower who has not made timely payments on his or her debt.

FRONT-END LOAD

A sales fee paid at the time an investment is purchased. This fee is deducted from the investment—thus lowering the size of the investment.

FUNDAMENTAL ANALYSIS

A method of evaluating securities that examines financial and economic factors—such as the current finances of a company and the prevailing economic environment—to determine whether the company's future value is accurately reflected in its current stock price.

GIFT

The voluntary transfer of assets under which the giver receives no compensation and retains no interest in his or her gift.

GIFT TAX

A tax the federal government and some states levy on the transfer of property as a gift. Generally gift taxes increase with the amount of the gift and are paid by the donor.

GROSS MONTHLY INCOME

Total monthly income generated from all sources before taxes and other expenses are considered.

GROUP LIFE INSURANCE

Life insurance that insures all the members of a specific group, most often the employees of a specific company or the members of a professional association.

HEALTH SAVINGS ACCOUNT (HSA)

An account that offers individuals covered by high-deductible health plans a tax-advantaged means to save for medical expenses. Within certain limits, funds contributed to the account are not subject to federal income taxes. Unlike Flexible Spending Accounts (FSAs), funds can be rolled over from year to year if not spent.

HOME EQUITY

The real value of a home after all liabilities have been paid. Thus a home worth $300,000 with a $200,000 mortgage would have $100,000 in equity.

INCOME

Monies or other compensation received from any source. This includes wages, commissions, bonuses, Social Security and other retirement benefits, unemployment compensation, disability, interest, and dividends. Generally, all income is taxable unless it is specifically exempted by law.

INDEX

An average of the prices of a hypothetical basket of securities representing a particular market or portion of a market. Among the most well known are the Dow Jones Industrials Index, or the Dow; the Standard & Poor's 500 Index, or the S&P 500; and the Russell 2000 Index. Index performance is not indicative of the past performance of a particular investment. Past performance does not guarantee future results. Individuals cannot invest directly in an index.

INDIVIDUAL RETIREMENT ACCOUNT (IRA)

A qualified retirement account for individuals. Contributions to a Traditional IRA may be fully or partially deductible, depending on your individual circumstance. Distributions from Traditional IRA and most other employer-sponsored retirement plans are taxed as ordinary income and, if taken before age 59½, may be subject to a 10% federal income tax penalty. Generally, once you reach age 70½, you must begin taking required minimum distributions.

INFLATION

An upward movement in the average level of prices. Each month, the Bureau of Labor Statistics reports on the average level of prices when it releases the Consumer Price Index (CPI).

INITIAL PUBLIC OFFERING (IPO)

A company's first public offering of stock. In an IPO, investment banks buy a company's shares and then offer them to the public at an offering price. As the stock is traded, the market price may be more or less than the offering price. Keep in mind that the return and principal value of stock prices will fluctuate as market conditions change. And shares, when sold, may be worth more or less than their original cost.

INTEREST RATE

The cost to borrow money expressed as a percentage of the loan amount over one year.

INTESTATE

The condition of an estate when its owner dies without leaving a valid will. In such circumstances, state law normally determines who inherits property and who serves as guardian for any minor children.

INVESTMENT OBJECTIVE

The stated financial goal of an investment.

IRREVOCABLE TRUST

A trust that cannot be altered, stopped, or canceled after its creation without the permission of the beneficiary or trustee. Using a trust involves a complex set of tax rules and regulations. Before moving forward with a trust, consider working with a professional who is familiar with the rules and regulations.

JOINT TENANCY

A form of property ownership under which two or more people have an undivided interest in the property and in which the survivor or survivors automatically assume ownership of the interest of any joint tenant who dies.

JOINTLY HELD PROPERTY

Property owned simultaneously by more than one person. All co-owners have an equal right to use the property, and no co-owner can exclude another co-owner from the property. The most common forms of jointly-held property are joint tenancy, tenancy in common, and, in some states, community property.

KEOGH PLAN

A tax-deferred retirement plan for self-employed individuals and employees of unincorporated businesses. Keogh plans are similar to IRAs but have significantly higher contribution limits. Distributions from Keogh plans and most other employer-sponsored retirement plans are taxed as ordinary income and, if taken before age 59½, may be subject to a 10% federal income tax penalty. Generally, once you reach age 70½, you must begin taking required minimum distributions.

KEY EMPLOYEE

An employee who has valuable skills, knowledge, or organizational abilities, who is considered critical to the success of a given company.

KEY PERSON INSURANCE

Company-owned insurance designed to cover the cost of replacing a key employee if he or she were to die or become disabled.

Life Insurance

A contract under which an insurance company promises, in exchange for premiums, to pay a set benefit when the policyholder dies. Several factors will affect the cost and availability of life insurance, including age, health and the type and amount of insurance purchased. Life insurance policies have expenses, including mortality and other charges. If a policy is surrendered prematurely, the policyholder also may pay surrender charges and have income tax implications. You should consider determining whether you are insurable before implementing a strategy involving life insurance. Any guarantees associated with a policy are dependent on the ability of the issuing insurance company to continue making claim payments.

LIQUIDITY

The ease and speed with which an asset or security can be bought or sold.

LIVING TRUST

A trust created by a living person which allows that person to control the assets he or she contributes to the trust during his or her lifetime and to direct their disposition upon his or her death.

LIVING WILL

A written document that allows the originator to designate someone to make medical decisions on his or her behalf in the event that he or she becomes incapacitated due to accident or illness.

LONG-TERM-CARE INSURANCE

Insurance that covers the cost of medical and non-medical services needed by those who have a chronic illness or disability—most commonly associated with aging. Long-term-care insurance can cover the cost of nursing home care, in-home assistance, assisted living, and adult day care.

LUMP-SUM DISTRIBUTION

A one-time payment of the entire amount held in an employer-sponsored retirement, pension plan, annuity, or similar account, rather than breaking payments into smaller installments.

MANAGEMENT FEE

The cost of having assets professionally managed. This fee is normally a fixed percentage of the fund's asset value; terms of the fee are disclosed in the prospectus.

MARITAL DEDUCTION

A provision of the tax code that allows an individual to transfer an unlimited amount of assets to his or her spouse at any time—including upon the individual's death—without triggering a tax liability.

MARKET RISK

The risk that an entire market will decline, reducing the value of the investments in it without regard to other factors. This is also known as Systemic Risk.

MARKET TIMING

An investment philosophy under which investors buy and sell securities in an attempt to profit from short-term price fluctuations.

MATURITY

The date on which a debt security comes due for payment and on which an investor's principal is due to be repaid.

MEDICAID

The federal government's health program for eligible individuals and families with low income and resources. It is means tested, meaning those who apply for benefits must demonstrate they have need.

MEDICARE

The federal government's health program for individuals aged 65 and over and for individuals who have certain disabilities or end-stage renal disease.

MONEY MARKET FUND

A mutual fund that invests in assets that are easily converted into cash and which have a low risk of price fluctuation. This may include money market holdings, Treasury bills, and commercial paper. Money held in money market funds is not insured or guaranteed by the Federal Deposit Insurance Corporation or any other government agency. Money market funds seek to preserve the value of your investment at $1.00 a share. However, it is possible to lose money by investing in a money market fund.

MUNICIPAL BOND

A debt security issued by a state, county, city, or other political entity (such as a school district) to raise public funds for special projects. The income from municipal bonds is normally exempt from federal income taxes. It may also be exempt from state income taxes in the state in which the municipal bond is issued. Bond prices rise and fall daily. Municipal bonds are subject to a variety of risks, including adjustments in interest rates, call risk, market conditions, and default risk. Some municipal bonds may be subject to the federal alternative minimum tax. When interest rates rise, bond prices generally will fall. Certain municipal bonds may be difficult to sell. A municipal bond issuer may be unable to make interest or principal payments, which may lead to the issuer defaulting on the bond. If this occurs, the municipal bond may have little or no value. If a bond is purchased at a premium, it may result in realized losses. It's possible that the interest on a municipal bond may be determined to be taxable after purchase.

MUNICIPAL BOND FUND

A mutual fund offered by an investment company which specifically invests in municipal bonds. Mutual fund balances are subject to fluctuation in value and market risk. Shares, when redeemed, may be worth more or less than their original cost. Mutual funds are sold only by prospectus. Individuals are encouraged to consider the charges, risks, expenses, and investment objectives carefully before investing. A prospectus containing this and other information about the investment company can be obtained from your financial professional. Read it carefully before you invest or send money.

MUTUAL FUND

A pooled investment account offered by an investment company. Mutual funds pool the monies of many investors and then invest the money to pursue the fund's stated objectives. The resulting portfolio of investments is managed by the investment company. Mutual fund balances are subject to fluctuation in value and market risk. Shares, when redeemed, may be worth more or less than their original cost. Mutual funds are sold only by prospectus. Individuals are encouraged to consider the charges, risks, expenses, and investment objectives carefully before investing. A prospectus containing this and other information about the investment company can be obtained from your financial professional. Read it carefully before you invest or send money.

NATIONAL ASSOCIATION OF SECURITIES DEALERS AUTOMATED QUOTATIONS (NASDAQ)

An American stock exchange originally founded by the National Association of Securities Dealers. When the NASDAQ stock exchange began trading on February 8, 1971, it was the world's first electronic stock market.

NET ASSET VALUE

The net market value of a mutual fund's current holdings divided by the number of outstanding shares. The product of this division estimates the per-share value of the fund's assets.

NET INCOME

A company's total revenues minus its costs, expenses, and taxes. Net income is the bottom line of a company's income statement (which may also be called the profit and loss statement).

NET WORTH

The value of a company's or individual's assets minus liabilities.

NEW YORK STOCK EXCHANGE (NYSE)

A stock exchange located on Wall Street in New York City, NY. Many regard the NYSE as the largest exchange in the U.S., and possibly in the world.

NON-CONTRIBUTORY RETIREMENT PLAN

A retirement plan that is funded entirely by employer contributions, with no employee contributions.

NON-QUALIFIED PLAN

A retirement or employee benefit plan that is not eligible for favorable tax treatment.

OLD-AGE, SURVIVORS, AND DISABILITY INSURANCE (OASDI)

The official name of the Social Security program. In addition to retirement benefits, it offers disability income, veterans' pensions, public housing, and food stamps.

PARTNERSHIP

A contract under which two or more individuals manage and operate a business venture.

PERMANENT LIFE INSURANCE

A class of life insurance policies that do not expire—as long as premiums are kept current—and which combine a death benefit with a savings component. This savings portion can accumulate a cash value against which the policy owner may be able to borrow funds. Several factors will affect the cost and availability of life insurance, including age, health and the type and amount of insurance purchased. Life insurance policies have expenses, including mortality and other charges. If a policy is surrendered prematurely, the policyholder also may pay surrender charges and have income tax implications. You should consider determining whether you are insurable before implementing a strategy involving life insurance. Any guarantees associated with a policy are dependent on the ability of the issuing insurance company to continue making claim payments.

POLICY LOAN

A loan made by an insurance company to a policyholder. Policy loans are secured by the cash value of a life insurance policy.

Withdrawals of earnings are fully taxable at ordinary income tax rates. If you are under age 59½ when you make the withdrawal, you may also be subject to a 10% federal income tax penalty. Also, withdrawals may reduce the benefits and value of the contract.

POLICY RIDER

A provision to a life insurance policy that is purchased separately from the basic policy and that provides additional benefits at additional cost.

POLICYHOLDER

The person or entity who holds an insurance policy; usually the client in whose name an insurance policy is written.

PORTFOLIO

The combined investments of an individual investor or mutual fund.

POWER OF ATTORNEY

A legal document that grants one person authority to act for another person in specific legal or financial matters in the event that said individual becomes incapacitated.

PREFERRED STOCK

Securities that represent ownership in a corporation and have a higher claim on a company's assets and earnings than common stock. Dividends on preferred stock are generally paid out before dividends to common stockholders.

PRENUPTIAL AGREEMENT

A contract entered into by those contemplating marriage that sets forth how their individual property will be divided should they ultimately divorce.

PRICE/EARNINGS RATIO (P/E RATIO)

A ratio calculated by dividing a stock's price by its earnings per share. Investors use this ratio to learn how much they are paying for a company's earnings.

PRIME INTEREST RATE

The interest rate commercial banks charge their most credit-worthy or "prime" customers. The prime interest rate is influenced by the federal funds rate.

PRINCIPAL

The original amount invested in a security, excluding earnings; the face value of a bond; or the remaining amount owed on a loan, separate from interest.

PROBATE

The court-supervised process in which a deceased person's debts are paid and any remaining assets distributed to his or her heirs.

PROPERTY

Anything over which a person or business has legal title. Property may be held in common or privately owned.

PROFIT-SHARING PLAN

A defined-contribution plan under which employees share in company profits. The funds within the plan accumulate tax deferred.

PROSPECTUS

A legal document that provides the information an investor needs to make an informed decision about an investment offered for sale to the public. Prospectuses are required by and filed with the Securities and Exchange Commission.

QUALIFIED RETIREMENT PLAN

A retirement plan that is established and operates within the rules laid down in Section 401(a) of the Internal Revenue Code, and thus receives favorable tax treatment.

RATE OF RETURN

A measure of the performance of an investment. Rate of return is calculated by dividing any gain or loss by an investment's initial cost. Rates of return usually account for any income received from the investment in addition to any realized capital gains.

REAL ESTATE INVESTMENT TRUST (REIT)

A pooled investment that invests primarily in real estate. REITs trade like stocks on the major exchanges. Keep in mind that the return and principal value of REIT prices will fluctuate as market conditions change. And shares, when sold, may be worth more or less than their original cost.

REDEMPTION

The return of an investor's principal in a debt security—such as a preferred stock or bond—upon maturity or cancellation by the entity that originally issued the security. Redemption can also refer to the sale of units in a mutual fund.

REQUIRED MINIMUM DISTRIBUTION (RMD)

The amount which must be withdrawn annually from a qualified retirement plan beginning April 1 of the year following the year in which the account holder reaches age 70½.

REVENUE

The amount of money a company brings in from its business activities during a given period, before expenses and taxes have been subtracted.

REVOCABLE TRUST

A trust that can be altered or canceled by its grantor. During the life of the trust, any income earned is distributed to the grantor; upon the grantor's death, the contents of the trust are transferred to its beneficiaries according to the terms of the trust.

RISK

The chance an investment will be lost or will provide less-than-expected returns.

RISK TOLERANCE

A measurement of an investor's willingness or ability to handle investment losses.

ROLLOVER

A tax-free transfer of assets from one qualified retirement program to another. Rollovers must be made in accordance with specific requirements to avoid a taxable event.

ROTH IRA

A qualified retirement plan in which earnings grow tax deferred and distributions are tax free. Contributions to a Roth IRA are generally not deductible for tax purposes, and there are income and contribution limits. Roth IRA contributions cannot be made by taxpayers with high incomes. To qualify for the tax-free and penalty-free withdrawal of earnings, Roth IRA distributions must meet a five-year holding requirement and occur after age 59½. Tax-free and penalty-free withdrawal also can be taken under certain other circumstances, such as after the owner's death. The original Roth IRA owner is not required to take minimum annual withdrawals.

ROTH IRA CONVERSION

The process of transferring assets from a traditional, SEP, or SIMPLE IRA to a Roth IRA. Roth IRA conversions are subject to specific requirements and may be taxable.

SECURITIES AND EXCHANGE COMMISSION (SEC)

A federal agency with a mandate to protect investors; to maintain fair, orderly, and efficient markets; and to facilitate capital formation. The SEC acts as one of the primary regulatory agencies for the investment industry.

SELF-DIRECTED IRA

An individual retirement arrangement in which the account holder can direct the investment of funds, subject to certain conditions and limits.

SHARE

A unit of ownership in a corporation or financial asset.

SAVINGS INCENTIVE MATCH PLAN FOR EMPLOYEES (SIMPLE)

A qualified retirement plan that allows employees and employers to contribute to traditional IRAs set up for employees. SIMPLE plans are available to small businesses—those with 100 or fewer employees—that do not currently offer another retirement plan.

SPLIT-DOLLAR PLAN

An arrangement under which an employer and employee share the obligations and benefits of a life insurance policy.

SPLIT-DOLLAR LIFE INSURANCE

An arrangement under which a life insurance policy's premium, cash values, and death benefit are split between two parties—usually a corporation and a key employee or executive. Under such an arrangement an employer may own the policy and pay the premiums and give a key employee or executive the right to name the recipient of the death benefit. Several factors will affect the cost and availability of life insurance, including age, health, and the type and amount of insurance purchased. Life insurance policies have expenses, including mortality and other charges. If a policy is surrendered prematurely, the policyholder also may pay surrender charges and have income tax implications. You should consider determining whether you are insurable before implementing a strategy involving life insurance. Any guarantees associated with a policy are dependent on the ability of the issuing insurance company to continue making claim payments.

SPOUSAL IRA

An individual retirement arrangement under which an IRA is established for a non-working spouse and is funded with contributions from the working spouse. Spousal and non-spousal IRAs are subject to combined annual contribution limits and must meet certain requirements. Contributions to a traditional IRA may be fully or partially deductible, depending on your individual circumstance. Distributions from traditional IRAs and most other employer-sponsored retirement plans are taxed as ordinary income and, if taken before age 59½, may be subject to a 10% federal income tax penalty. Generally, once you reach age 70½, you must begin taking required minimum distributions.

STANDARD & POOR'S 500 INDEX (S&P 500)

An average calculated by summing the prices of 500 leading companies in leading industries of the U.S. economy and dividing the sum by a divisor which is regularly adjusted to account for stock splits, spinoffs, or similar structural changes. Index performance is not indicative of the past performance of a particular investment. Past performance does not guarantee future results. Individuals cannot invest directly in an index.

STOCK

An equity investment in a company. Stockholders own a share of the company and are entitled to any dividends and financial participation in company growth. They also have the right to vote on the company's board of directors. Keep in mind that the return and principal value of stock prices will fluctuate as market conditions change. And shares, when sold, may be worth more or less than their original cost.

STOCK CERTIFICATE

A legal document that certifies ownership of a specific number of shares of stock in a corporation. In many transactions, the stockholder is registered electronically, and no certificate is issued.

STOCK PURCHASE PLAN

A program under which an employer offers its employees the opportunity to buy stock at a favorable price, often through payroll deduction.

STOCK SPLIT

A decision by a company to increase the number of shares of stock it has outstanding by issuing more shares to its current shareholders. For example, in a 2-for-1 split each shareholder would receive as many new shares as he or she owns—effectively doubling the number of shares he or she owns. The price per share adjusts to account for the split. In the example of a 2-for-1 split, each of the new shares would have a par value of half the prior price.

TAX CREDIT

A credit subtracted from income taxes after preliminary tax liability has been calculated.

TAX DEDUCTION

An amount that can be subtracted from a taxpayer's income before taxes are calculated. Taxpayers may use the standard deduction or may itemize deductions if allowable itemized deductions exceed the standard deduction.

TAX DEFERRED

A condition of certain plans and accounts under which the funds in the plan or account along with any accrued interest, dividends, or other capital gains, are not subject to taxes until the funds are withdrawn.

TAX-EXEMPT BONDS

Debt securities issued by a state, county, city, or other political entity (such as a school district) that generate income which is exempt from federal income taxes. Income from such bonds may also be exempt from state income taxes in the state in which the bond is issued. However, some tax-exempt bonds may be subject to the federal alternative minimum tax. Bond prices rise and fall daily. Municipal bonds are subject to a variety of risks, including adjustments in interest rates, call risk, market conditions, and default risk. When interest rates rise, bond prices generally will fall. Certain municipal bonds may be difficult to sell. A municipal bond issuer may be unable to make interest or principal payments, which may lead to the issuer defaulting on the bond. If this occurs, the municipal bond may have little or no value. If a bond is purchased at a premium, it may result in realized losses. It's possible that the interest on a municipal bond may be determined to be taxable after purchase.

TAXABLE INCOME

A taxpayer's gross income, minus any adjustments, itemized deductions or the standard deduction, and personal exemptions. Taxable income is used to compute tax liability.

TECHNICAL ANALYSIS

A method of evaluating securities by examining recent price movements and trends in an attempt to identify patterns that can suggest future activity. Generally, technical analysis is the opposite of fundamental analysis.

TENANCY IN COMMON

A form of property ownership under which two or more people have an undivided interest in the property and in which the interest of a deceased owner passes to his or her beneficiaries rather than to the surviving owners.

TERM INSURANCE

Life insurance that provides coverage for a specific period. If the policyholder dies during that time, his or her beneficiaries receive the benefit from the policy. If the policyholder outlives the term of the policy, it is no longer in effect. Several factors will affect the cost and availability of life insurance, including age, health, and the type and amount of insurance purchased.

Life insurance policies have expenses, including mortality and other charges. If a policy is surrendered prematurely, the policyholder also may pay surrender charges and have income tax implications. You should consider determining whether you are insurable before implementing a strategy involving life insurance. Any guarantees associated with a policy are dependent on the ability of the issuing insurance company to continue making claim payments.

TESTAMENTARY TRUST

A trust created by a will or trust that is established on the death of the trustor. Using a trust involves a complex set of tax rules and regulations. Before moving forward with a trust, consider working with a professional who is familiar with the rules and regulations.

TIME HORIZON

The amount of time an investor plans to hold an investment or portfolio of investments.

TITLE

A legal document that serves as evidence of ownership of an asset or security.

TOTAL RETURN

The total of all earnings from an investment or portfolio, including both capital appreciation and any income received.

TREASURIES

Debt securities issued by the United States government. Treasury bills normally have maturities of less than one year, while Treasury notes have maturities between one and 10 years, and Treasury bonds have maturities between 10 and 30 years. U.S. Treasury securities are guaranteed by the federal government as to the timely payment of principal and interest. However, if you sell a Treasury security prior to maturity, it could be worth more or less than the original price paid.

TRUST

A trust is a legal arrangement that creates a separate entity which can own property and is managed for the benefit of a beneficiary. A living trust is created while its grantor is still alive. A testamentary trust is created upon the grantor's death—usually by another trust or by a will. Using a trust involves a complex set of tax rules and regulations. Before moving forward with a trust, consider working with a professional who is familiar with the rules and regulations.

TRUSTEE

An individual, corporation, or other entity that manages property held in a trust.

TRUSTEE-TO-TRUSTEE TRANSFER

A means for transferring assets from one qualified retirement program to another without triggering a taxable event.

UNIFORM GIFT TO MINORS ACT (UGMA)

An act available in some states that allows assets to be held in a custodian's name for the benefit of a minor without the need to set up a trust. Once the child to whom the assets have been gifted reaches the age of maturity in his or her state, the assets become his or her property and can be used for any purpose.

UNIVERSAL LIFE INSURANCE

Permanent life insurance that allows the policyholder to vary the amount and timing of premiums and, by extension, the death benefit. Universal life insurance policies accumulate cash value which grows tax deferred. Several factors will affect the cost and availability of life insurance, including age, health, and the type and amount of insurance purchased. Life insurance policies have expenses, including mortality and other charges. If a policy is surrendered prematurely, the policyholder also may pay surrender charges and have income tax implications. You should consider determining whether you are insurable before implementing a strategy involving life insurance. Any guarantees associated with a policy are dependent on the ability of the issuing insurance company to continue making claim payments.

UNLIMITED MARITAL DEDUCTION

A provision of the tax code that allows an individual to transfer an unlimited amount of assets to his or her spouse at any time—including upon the individual's death—without triggering a tax liability.

VARIABLE INTEREST RATE

An interest rate that moves up and down with a specific measure or index, such as current money market rates or a lender's cost of funds.

VARIABLE UNIVERSAL LIFE INSURANCE

Permanent life insurance that allows the policyholder to vary the amount and timing of premiums and, by extension, the death benefit. Universal life insurance policies accumulate cash value which grows tax deferred. Within certain limits, policyholders can direct how this cash value will be allocated among subaccounts offered within the policy. Several factors will affect the cost and availability of life insurance, including age, health, and the type and amount of insurance purchased. Life insurance policies have expenses, including mortality and other charges. If a policy is surrendered prematurely, the policyholder also may pay surrender charges and have income tax implications. You should consider determining whether you are insurable before implementing a strategy involving life insurance. Any guarantees associated with a policy are dependent on the ability of the issuing insurance company to continue making claim payments.

VOLATILITY

A measure of the range of potential fluctuations in a security's value. A higher volatility means the security's value can potentially fluctuate over a larger range of potential outcomes—up and down.

WHOLE LIFE INSURANCE

Permanent life insurance with fixed premiums and death benefit. Whole life insurance policies accumulate cash value which grows tax deferred. Several factors will affect the cost and availability of life insurance, including age, health, and the type and amount of insurance purchased. Life insurance policies have expenses, including mortality and other charges. If a policy is surrendered prematurely, the policyholder also may pay surrender charges and have income tax implications.

You should consider determining whether you are insurable before implementing a strategy involving life insurance. Any guarantees associated with a policy are dependent on the ability of the issuing insurance company to continue making claim payments.

WILL

A legal document by which an individual or a couple identifies their wishes regarding the distribution of their assets after death as well as the guardianship of any minor children.

WITHHOLDING

The process by which an employer holds back part of an employee's compensation to pay his or her share of income, Social Security, and Medicare taxes. Amounts withheld are paid to the IRS in the employee's name.

YIELD

A measure of the performance of an investment. Yield is calculated by dividing the income received from an investment by the investment's initial cost. Yield differs from rate of return in that it accounts only for income; rate of return also includes appreciation or depreciation in the value of the investment.

Zero-Coupon Bond

A bond that does not pay interest during its life. Zero-coupon bonds are purchased at a discount from their face value. When a zero-coupon bond matures, the investor receives the face value of the bond. The market value of a bond will fluctuate with changes in interest rates. As rates rise, the value of existing bonds typically falls. If an investor sells a bond before maturity, it may be worth more or less that the initial purchase price. By holding a bond to maturity, an investor will receive the interest payments due plus his or her original principal, barring default by the issuer. Investments seeking to achieve higher yields also involve a higher degree of risk. Bond prices rise and fall daily. Bonds are subject to a variety of risks, including adjustments in interest rates, call risk, market conditions, and default risk. When interest rates rise, bond prices generally will fall. Certain municipal bonds may be difficult to sell. A bond issuer may be unable to make interest or principal payments, which may lead to the issuer defaulting on the bond. If this occurs, the bond may have little or no value. If a bond is purchased at a premium, it may result in realized losses. It's possible that the interest on a municipal bond may be determined to be taxable after purchas

Made in the USA
San Bernardino, CA
21 January 2018